Territorial Spirits

Insights on Strategic-Level
Spiritual Warfare
from
Nineteen Christian Leaders

Edited by C. Peter Wagner

Sovereign World Limited

Sovereign World Ltd
P.O. Box 17
Chichester
England PO20 6YB

British Library Cataloguing in Publication Data
Wagner, C. Peter (Charles Peter) 1930–
    Territorial spirits.
    1. Evil
    I. Title
    234.5

    ISBN 1-85240-055-2

Typeset by CRB Typesetting Services, Ely, Cambs.
Printed by Richard Clay Ltd, Bungay, Suffolk.

*This book
is affectionately dedicated
to
George and Pam Marhad
cherished partners in ministry*

Contents

Foreword

by Roger Forster

It is a privilege to be alive in these exciting times; times of recovering God's truth and completing the mission of the church. It is also a privilege to write the foreword for this strategic book, compiled by Peter Wagner. First, because it means that I may put my modest contribution alongside those of men and women of high spiritual calibre who have contributed to this symposium of excellent material! This material comes from their personal experiences in the subject and not from any ivory towers of theoretical inquiry. To understand truth thoroughly it must be participated in and these writers have done that. Secondly, because it provides the opportunity to contribute a little to the ongoing inquiry into and recovery of this important subject of spiritual warfare.

I am trying in the foreword to add a few dimensions not yet addressed in the ongoing chapters. In this I am very concious that more research, debate and experience will yet be needed to lay hold of God's mind more completely on this crucial subject. We are, as the church of Christ, having to rediscover the Bible world view of spirits and angels, principalities and powers, which has been lost by years of materialistic interpretations and demythologising. We are having to resurrect Bible language to account for a genuine dimension in our human experience of reality, especially, it would seem, in our experience of evil, which is unaccounted for by rationalistic, materialistic, secular philosophies and theologies. It is reported that C.G. Jung, one of the founding fathers of modern psychology, said words to the effect that in the absence of an adequate terminology we must resurrect the category of demons. This was just after World War II and he recognised that our 20th century vocabulary had lost the ability to speak adequately of the appalling expressions of evil that that catastrophic war had thrown up. In the wake of the collapse of the Nazi regime, Jung went on to refer to Matthew 8:28–34 and the Gaderene demoniac, pointing out that when a devil is cast out he goes somewhere else (Essays on Contemporary Events. C.G. Jung). In the Mark account of this story we notice that even then the demon was reluctant to leave the territory altogether – *'And he began to entreat Him earnestly not to send them out of the country.'* (Mark 5:10 NASB)

It would be sad if we who love and trust the Bible should prove to be too slow, lazy, or even blinded by contemporary secular thinking, to serve our generation and advance God's Kingdom in providing an understanding in this important subject.

Without doubt the Bible presents us with a theology of battle, that is spiritual battle. In the first pages of Genesis we read *'I will put enmity between you* (Satan) *and the woman, and between your seed and her seed; he shall bruise you on the head, and you shall bruise him on the heel'* (Genesis 3:15 NASB). This opens the war between Satan and the woman's seed, evil and good, sin and salvation. Thousands of years later Jesus reasserts this basic enmity and initiates a new level of engagement with his declaration of war *'Repent, the Kingdom of Heaven is at hand'*. His assertation is confidently made in the face of the kingdom of darkness and the prince of death (Matthew 4:12–17) *'... The people who were sitting in darkness saw a great light, and to those who were sitting in the land and shadow of death, upon them a light dawned... '* (v.16 NASB). This follows the defeat of that enemy commander through Jesus' personal engagement with him in the wilderness (Matthew 4:1-11). The last great battle of this age-long conflict is recorded in Revelation 19:11–21 – the battle of Armageddon (Revelation 16:14–16). This is the final overthrow of endemic, structural and personal evil in this age. The Biblical world view, along with all other Bible doctrines, only makes satisfactory and adequate sense in the light of battle theology.

A unilateral declaration of independence (UDI) was declared by Satan (an angel of light – Lucifer, lit. *'star of the morning, son of the dawn'* Isaiah 14:12 NASB) when he rebelled against God's government. The rebellion involved the structures created and established by God's central creatorial government. These are created good as is all of God's creation, Genesis 1:31. If we compare the earthly parallel, a revolutionary leader can not rebel effectively without using structures such as the police, government officers, military and local government departments, that is, structures established by the original government; similarly Satan also needs to take other spiritual forces with him to effect his opposition to God, whether they go willingly or unwillingly. These principalities and powers sometimes appear as incorrigibly wicked but at other times they are called upon to repent or at least to do better. *'God presides in the great assembly; He gives judgement among the gods. "How long will you defend the unjust and show partiality to the wicked? Defend the cause of the weak and fatherless.. "'* (Psalm 82 NIV). To answer the question whether these forces who are addressed as 'gods' (Psalm 82:6) are implacably evil or not, possibly needs *'more light yet to break forth from God's word'*.

It seems that Satan is allowed to continue to oppose God, not because of some dualism of equal power between good and evil – namely God and the devil – but rather because of the creator's predicament on account of Satan's rebellion. In a human situation the central government could resolve the problems of the UDI by its superior force and bring about the total destruction of the colony. Of course, God could dismiss and dethrone Satan in that way, but all the creation – angels, men and the world around us – would disintegrate with that same exertion of power. Alternatively He might allow the structures to remain in the colony, supporting life and order, while negotiations and sanctions are brought to bear, and a resistance movement is set up. This alternative solution necessitates allowing Satan and other spiritual powers to continue in their God-appointed offices, even though they are basically in opposition to the purposes of God, while God forbears to use destructive solutions to restore normality. This is why Satan is seen both serving God's purposes as His agent – 2 Samuel 24:1; 1 Chronicles 21:1; Luke 22:31 and opposing Him as an adversary – Job 1 & 2; 1 Peter 3:8. Eventually, the resistance movement can produce sufficient numbers of trained personnel to take over the authority and administration of the colony from Satan and his angels, giving the least amount of disturbance to the heavenly structural powers. Since through these powers Christ holds the universe together, this procedure would ultimately complete what God originally intended for His creation. Instead of utterly dismissing the universe into oblivion because of its rebellion and starting over again, God still pursues his original purpose. The idyllic conditions of the garden in Genesis 2 are developed into the garden city of Revelation chapters 21 and 22.

Hebrews 2:5 reveals to us that the world to come will no longer be under subjection to angels but will be under subjection to redeemed men and women who will reign with Christ. We at present are in training for reigning (2 Timothy 2:12; 1 Corinthians 6:2–3; Romans 8:17). The structures will be refurbished with a whole new personnel. The final overthrow of Satan's rebellious colonial government by the central government of God is preceded by the faith-sons of Abraham bringing blessing to all the families of the earth. This demands territorial claims and advance through the earth. The church is to preach the gospel in all the world *'for a witness to all nations and then the end shall come'* (Matthew 24:14 NASB). Until such a network of resistance against Satan is found all over the earth the second coming of our Lord is held up and his total reign restrained (c.f. 2 Peter 3:12). Jesus already has all authority in heaven and earth (Matthew 28:18–20), but this authority is not yet expressed totally on earth. The expression of his Kingdom on earth comes through the church but is hindered by evil spiritual forces, as well as our unbelief. Structural spirit forces of society holding ground from God are one form of this hindrance. These territorial spirits hold ground from God who first ordained their existence and territory. A number of writers in this book refer to Deuteronomy 32:8, Psalm 82 and Daniel 7–12, where nations or city states are viewed from the point of view of their spirit powers. Again may I suggest there is more biblical understanding in these matters yet to grasp.

For instance, the internal solidarity of Sodom or Babylon is affected by powers that bind people together. Similarly, the solidarity of the resistance movement, the church, is the unity of the Holy Spirit. The Holy Spirit may also act territorially, for example at Pentecost, when he came to an area in Jerusalem, rather than to Bethlehem or Nazareth. Of course God's Spirit is omnipresent but He still manifests himself – pentecostal wise – in regions or places. It was said that you could feel the love of God a quarter of a mile around the Azusa Street Mission in 1906 in the U.S.A. when the Holy Spirit moved there. During the Welsh revival in 1904 a little girl in a North Welsh town said 'it is Sunday every day now that Jesus has come to live in our town'.

The purpose of the church is to be the instrument of the Holy Spirit's territorial manifestation. This manifestation is the Kingdom of God, as illustrated in Matthew 12:28, where Jesus in his incarnate body releases the Holy Spirit into the events and circumstances of his immediate area and says *'if I cast out demons by the Spirit of God, then the Kingdom of God has come upon you'* (NASB). God's Kingdom is, *'Justice, peace and joy in the Holy Spirit'* (Romans 14:17 NIV), and, of course, His will being *'done on earth as it is in heaven'* (Matthew 6:10). While the church, the new body of Christ, is seeking to bring in the Kingdom, we inevitably will be confronted by the opposing kingdom of spirits, angels, gods, principalities, powers and thrones. These are employed by Satan, in their appointed territories, to bind, blind and buffet the inhabitants.

In the Old Testament God's people were to inherit the territory of Canaan. Even when the whole land was captured, pockets of Canaanite opposition continued and from time to time were dominant or rose up and reinhabited defeated cities. At other times outside enemies took the land and its resources from Israel. This was usually when the Baals and Asteroths, who were linked to the land, were worshipped, as in Judges 6:6–10, 25–6, 31–2. Joshua and Judges in particular tell the story of the declines and the revivals of the fortunes of God's people as they lost or regained territory. Eventually David's reign subdues all opposition and the kingdom of Solomon (peace) ensues. In those days there were two understandings of the inheritance: (1) *God himself* – as the Levites emphasised by having no earthly inheritance (Numbers 18:20). (2) *Territory of Canaan itself* with its enemies to destroy and subdue. Today the inheritance is also two-fold: (1) *God in Christ* – whose body we inherit and participate in as we feed daily on him (Luke 18:18, 23:19; Ephesians 1:11, 14, 18). (2) *The territory of the world* (Matthew 5:5 NIV) *'the humble shall inherit the earth'* – *'this good news shall be preached in all the world'* (Matthew 24:14 NIV) – *'the kingdom of this world has become the Kingdom of our Lord and of His Christ'* (Revelation 11:15 NIV). Both inheritances will be contested by Satan and his spirit powers. Both must be laid hold of while keeping them in balance or proportion with each other (see Peter Wagner's article and the helpful graph, page 26). The inheritance is both our inner inheritance through which we get deeper and deeper into God and his resources in Christ, and our outer inheritence which is the world claimed through evangelism in all its forms of words, works and wonders. These two aspects of inheriting must be pursued together, and they must be pursued despite the opposition of the enemy.

If at last the great commission is being fulfilled then inevitably the church must also at last be coming up to both the *'measure of the stature of the fulness of Christ'* and to *'the knowledge of the Son of God'* (Ephesians 4:13). Evidently the church of Paul's day was not at this point yet, but was still moving on. I believe with all my heart that the rediscovery, or perhaps it is the re-emphasis, of territorial spirits is a part of God's desire and design to get his people into the full knowledge of the Son of God so that we can grow to the full stature, geographically and territorially, as well as powerfully and inwardly, and that this will enable us to fulfil the world mission of the church.

It is significant that angelic gods for the nations in Psalm 82 are addressed not only by God but by the prophetic psalmist also, saying that they should submit to God's way and only then is this followed by the prayer *'Arise, O God, judge the earth! For it is You who possesses all the nations'*. Nations who will one day be brought to judgement, as in Matthew 24:32, are first approached by addressing their respective angelic principalities.

Many times in our inner city evangelism we are aware that we have touched, disturbed, engaged and at times overturned spiritual forces involved in the solidarities of different areas and sections of society. Also we are aware that at times we are touching the spirit of the city or even the nation. These are the powers we must cast out and overcome if we are to see captives released, especially in huge revival numbers. Indeed revival seems to occur whenever these forces are rendered innocuous (Daniel 7:12), or even made to serve instead of hinder the gospel. In a completely unevangelised territory, the gospel will often hit the power structures in an unguarded place and we see society turned around to Jesus in a dramatic way. In Europe however (and in some other places) we have the difficulty of a 'post Christian' society. This is where society has been won over in the past and the spirit forces overcome or cast out, but then the ground has not been held by the church through faith and prayer and holy living. Gradually the opposition has mustered strength again and re-taken the ground as happened in the Old Testament when the Jebusites re-occupied Jerusalem. Jesus himself taught that when an evil spirit is cast out of a house it will return if the place is not occupied and on its return will bring seven worse spirits with it. This is surely the case in Europe today where it is much harder to see the Kingdom advance than in many completely pagan nations.

As we have already seen, it must not be overlooked that when God addresses the spirits in Psalm 82, he uses the psalmist as a prophet to address them. (Similarly, in Revelation chapters 2 and 3, John is instructed to prophesy to the 'angels' of the churches.) If it is true that *'the Lord God does nothing unless He reveals His secret counsel to His servants the prophets'* (Amos 3:7 NASB), then one of the major functions of the prophetic church is to listen to God and prophesy to the powers as well as the people when we are seeking to take or re-take ground for God.

Moreover, the only two mentions of the word 'church' in the gospels describe its function as locking or unlocking (binding and loosing) with the Kingdom keys (Matthew 16:18–19; 18:17–20). What kind of church is it, we may ask, which never engages in this primary activity of its calling and is not teaching its members to reign now in Christ so that they will reign with Christ in the future age? (c.f. also Matthew 12:28–30; Luke 13:16).

God has given me a vision from the dragnet parable in Matthew 13:47–50, *'Again the Kingdom of heaven is like a dragnet cast into the sea, and gathering fish of every kind; and when it was filled, they drew it up on the beach; and they sat down, and gathered the good fish into containers, but the bad they threw away. So it will be at the end of the age; the angels shall come forth, and take out the wicked from among the righteous, and will cast them into the furnace of fire; there shall be weeping and gnashing of teeth.'* Everything, good and bad, is caught in it and only then is it pulled in and the evil cast out. Jesus will pull in the net of his Kingdom when it covers the world, enmeshing everything, good and evil. When the evil has been removed the fullness of the Kingdom will come and be seen (Revelation 11:15). Till that day arrives our task is to network the world. Each local church is like a knot in the net from which it extends, emits and exerts Holy Spirit Kingdom power over the immediate territory, till it links to the next knot (church) and so on through the earth. Evil will be there in great evidence too, but enmeshed and ready for the judgement haul-in.

No wonder the territorial spirits will resist with all their ability, no wonder God is revealing to us their activity today. Both things call for men and women to learn how to reign, since they herald the final demise of the kingdom of darkness, the final completion of world evangelisation and the final cry for our Lord's return, Maranatha! The end, or rather the beginning, comes. We then shall be '... *heirs of God and fellow heirs with Christ, if indeed we suffer with him in order that we may also be glorified with Him'* (Romans 8:17 NASB). What a destiny!

As you go further into this book, my prayer to the Father of all spirits, through Christ the head of every principality and power, and by the seven-fold Spirit of God, is that you will be inspired as I have been by its chapters to go further into God and into his world to complete the mission of the church.

Roger T. Forster
January 1991

Introduction

by C. Peter Wagner

The growing interest among scholars, pastors, missionaries, evangelists, and lay Christians in strategic-level spiritual warfare cries out for research and teaching. Many, myself included, have begun to make efforts to respond to this need.

Soon after I began to build a reference library on the issues of territorial spirits and intercessory prayer against wicked principalities and powers, it occurred to me that I was locating bits and pieces of important information which many of the Christian leaders who needed it most would be hard-pressed to know about or to locate even if they did. Thus, the idea of putting together a book such as this one.

Some of the material is from out-of-print sources, some from periodicals which may have been discarded long ago, and some from a variety of books still in print which I highly recommend to readers who wish further information. The only original, unpublished material is my Chapter 1 'Spiritual Warfare,' and Vernon J. Sterk's Chapter 16, 'Territorial Spirits and Evangelization in Hostile Environments.'

Now that this material has been put together for the first time, it constitutes a book which I believe is unique in Christian literature. I took the pains to examine the 100 (it happened to be an exact number) books listed in the Fuller Theological

Seminary McAlister Library card catalog under 'angelology' and 'demonology.' Of the 100 books only 5 so much as mentioned the issue of territoriality. Of the 5 which did, only 3 had information which could be regarded as helpful, but none was valuable enough to include in this volume. Spiritual territoriality has not been a prominent issue for theologians and biblical scholars through the years, at least for some 95 percent of them.

You can expect to read material from authors from many different backgrounds and using many different styles. We have journalists, pastors, professors, missionaries, biblical scholars, anthropologists, and itinerant preachers. While most of the material has been previously published in the United States, the authors include an Argentine, a Korean, a Zimbabwean, a German, a New Zealander, and two Britons, as well as Americans.

This variety is reflected in many ways. For one thing, not all of the authors will agree with each other on the details, although all will agree that our primary battle for the evangelization of the world is spiritual, involving spiritual warfare with high-ranking principalities and powers. Some come from an evangelical perspective, and some from a charismatic perspective. We have Lutherans, Baptists, Congregationalists, Pentecostals, Presbyterians, Anglicans, Reformed, and Mennonites just to name some. Naturally, the items will vary in forms of punctuation, capitalization, referencing, and spelling. I regret that some were written before many of us became aware of the need to use gender inclusive language, but I have not seen fit to attempt to edit out the discriminatory language of older days.

It is my prayer that God will use this book to inform, motivate, and equip vast numbers of committed Christians who are prepared to accept God's invitation to enlist in the mighty spiritual army He is raising up so that in cities and nations across the globe God's kingdom will come and His will be done on earth as it is in heaven.

Part I

THE ISSUES:

Principles and Problems

1

Spiritual Warfare

by C. Peter Wagner

As we begin moving into the 1990s, I sense, along with many other Christian leaders, that the Holy Spirit is saying, 'Prepare for warfare.' This decade may see the most intense spiritual warfare of recent times. We may see some of the greatest victories for God and His kingdom, and we may see some of the most serious setbacks. The final outcome, however, is not in doubt. The power of Satan was definitively broken on the cross and it may well be that the enemy knows the end is near and that he is waging a last ditch stand which will end at Armageddon.

This is not happening in a vacuum. Through recent decades God has been moving His people, step by step, through phases of preparation, setting the agenda for the current decade. As I analyze the trends, I believe that in 1950 God began to ripen the greatest spiritual harvest in all of Christian history and He put evangelism at home and in the world high on our agendas. In 1960 God began speaking to us about compassion for the poor, the oppressed, the homeless and the destitute. Social responsibility was added to the agenda. In 1970 we saw the first seeds of what is developing now into the greatest prayer movement in living memory. In 1980 a contemporary renewal of the prophetic ministry began and, while this is not so widely recognized as yet, the gift of prophecy and the office of prophet are reemerging. Now in 1990 spiritual warfare is moving to the forefront.

To go further back in the historical context, the holiness movement of the late 1800s and the Pentecostal movement of the early 1900s laid foundations for personal righteousness on one hand and ministry with supernatural signs and wonders on the other. Both of these have continued to play major roles in preparing the church for the 1990s. I believe we will see increasing emphasis on both holiness and power ministries in the years to come.

Is 'Warfare' the Best Term?

I wish we didn't have to think about this phase of ministry as 'warfare.' After all, Christians are not advocates of war. Jesus is known as the Prince of Peace.

If I personally were to choose an analogy for our struggle with the enemy, I might want to say it is like a football game. I could think of many very descriptive parallels between football and our adversarial relationship with Satan. This would be much more pleasant than talking in militaristic terms.

But I am not free to do this. The Bible itself describes our fight against the devil as warfare. And I believe the reason for this is clear. We are in a life and death struggle. Football games are intense while they are being played, but very few people can remember who held the national championship two years ago. It doesn't make that much difference. But, unlike football, our spiritual struggle bears eternal consequences. It can mean the difference between heaven and hell for millions of people. Warfare is not a game. There is a finality to war unlike any other human activity.

God's Kingdom Implies Tribulation

The apostle Paul says, 'We must through many tribulations enter the kingdom of God' (Acts 14:22). On several occasions he details what some of this tribulation can be expected to look like. He says that perilous times will come and people will arise who are lovers of themselves, lovers of money, blasphemers, disobedient to parents, unloving, unforgiving, brutal and despisers of good (see 2 Tim. 3:1–5). He speaks of the persecutions that he suffered, and says, 'All who desire to live godly lives in Christ Jesus will suffer persecutions' (2 Tim. 3:10–12). He desires that we 'be counted worthy of the kingdom of God, for which you also suffer' (2 Thess. 1:5). He was physically driven out of city after city and stoned to death in one of them.

Satan is referred to several times as the god of this age or the prince of the power of the air. He has usurped God's authority and set up his kingdom here on earth. His power is awesome. Luther insightfully said, 'On earth is not his equal.'

When Jesus came He invaded Satan's kingdom with the kingdom of God. Satan was not only insulted, but his power was broken through the death and resurrection of Jesus Christ. He is not taking this invasion lying down. That is why violence has erupted both in the heavenlies and here on earth. That is why Jesus said, 'The kingdom of heaven suffers violence and the violent take it by force' (Matt. 11:12). That is why Paul said, 'We must through many tribulations enter the kingdom of God.'

As we enter the kingdom of God we can choose one of two postures. We can draw back and protect ourselves in a defensive posture or we can move forward aggressively in an offensive posture. Those who choose the defensive will attempt to avoid spiritual warfare. Many I know even get upset when others talk about it. I agree with what John Dawson says in his book, *Taking Our Cities for God* (Creation House): 'We need to lift ourselves out of a self-centered spirituality – a mentality that says we are victims rather than warriors' (p. 21).

Jesus Changed the Picture

I mentioned that Jesus came to invade Satan's kingdom. When He did, the long period of time covered by the Old Testament

5

permanently changed. Jesus brought a new covenant.

When precisely did things change? Theologically, they changed on the cross. Paul explains this in some detail in Colossians when he says that the Father 'has delivered us from the power of darkness and translated us into the kingdom of the Son of His love' (Col. 1:13). He then goes on to say that we have redemption through His blood (see Col. 1:14). The blood that Jesus shed on the cross defeated the enemy, or as Paul later says, 'having disarmed principalities and powers, He made a public spectacle of them, triumphing over them in it' (Col. 2:15). He declares that Jesus is the 'head of all principality and power' (Col. 2:10).

The *de jure* defeat of Satan came on the cross. However, a *de facto* power encounter occurred earlier which served notice to Satan that he was through. Jesus said that John the Baptist was a great person, 'but he who is least in the kingdom of heaven is greater than he. And from the days of John the Baptist until now the kingdom of heaven suffers violence and the violent take it by force' (Matt. 11:11–12). How could Jesus declare this before he went to the cross? He could declare it because he had met Satan head on in the wilderness. Jesus' temptation was a high-level power encounter which Satan conclusively lost.

Notice that Jesus from the start took the offensive posture. The first thing that happened after His baptism was that He was 'led up by the Spirit into the wilderness to be tempted by the devil' (Matt. 4:1). This episode of spiritual warfare took place at God's initiative. Jesus, of course, was victorious. And we also can be victorious as we are united with Him and allow His power to flow through us.

Four Key Dimensions to Spiritual Warfare

Spiritual warfare is not fun and games. It is not some kids running around in devil costumes on Halloween or a spooky horror movie on television. These may be part of it, but they are nothing more than masquerades of the real thing. Satan and the demons under his control are real beings with warped personalities, wicked hearts and malicious intents. They are more powerful than humans, but they are not God nor anywhere near to God. We are not suggesting a new form of dualism. In fact, God is their creator just as He is ours. Even though their power is limited, and even though God has given us authority over them, a chief danger in spiritual warfare is to be overconfident. Many Christians have been clobbered spiritually, emotionally and physically because they have not been wise in their approach.

In approaching spiritual warfare wisely, there are four dimensions which must be carefully considered: 1) our weapons of warfare; 2) our spiritual authority; 3) our engagement with the enemy; 4) our plan of action. Let's look at them one at a time.

1. Our Weapons of Warfare

I have found by personal experience that one of the most difficult lessons for the average Christian to learn is that our weapons for spiritual warfare are spiritual weapons. It sounds simple, and it is in theory. But it is difficult in practice because even those of us who are biblical Christians still live much too much of our lives in the flesh.

The Bible is clear. 'For though we walk in the flesh, we do not war according to the flesh. For the weapons of our warfare are not carnal but mighty in God for pulling down strongholds' (2 Cor. 10:3–4). We are so used to trying to solve social and economic problems through politics, or legal problems through the courts, or personal disagreements through arguing about them, or international relationships through war, that to hear that God has a higher and more effective way through spiritual weapons is regarded as wishful thinking, even by many born-again Christians. This attitude needs to change.

What, then, are the weapons of our warfare?

The central, foundational activity for spiritual warfare is prayer. In one sense prayer is a weapon of warfare, and in another sense it is the medium through which all of the other weapons are utilized. A chief New Testament passage on spiritual warfare is Ephesians 6 where we are told that 'We do not wrestle against flesh and blood, but against principalities, against powers, against the rulers of the darkness of this age, against spiritual hosts of wickedness in the heavenly places' (Eph. 6:12). We are told to put on the full armor of God, 'praying always with all prayer and supplication in the Spirit' (Eph. 6:18). Without prayer we are impotent in our struggle with the enemy.

If prayer is the central *activity* for spiritual warfare, the central *attitude* for those of us in the battle is faith and obedience. At one point when Jesus was on earth, His disciples tried to cast a demon out of an epileptic boy and could not. After Jesus stepped in, cast out the demon and healed the boy, the disciples asked Him why they couldn't do it. Jesus said, 'Because of your unbelief' (Matt. 17:20). The disciples lacked the faith to succeed in that episode of spiritual warfare. Jesus tried to encourage them by telling them that as their faith increases they will have the power to move mountains, and 'nothing will be impossible for you' (Matt. 17:20).

What does faith do? For one thing, through faith we establish our relationship to God. We are saved by grace through faith (Eph. 2:8). Then once we are in fellowship with God, we move on from there to deepen our relationship with the Father through faith. That is why Ephesians 6 lists a part of the full armor of God as 'the shield of faith' (Eph. 6:16).

Faith cannot be understood apart from obedience to God. How do we know if we really have the kind of faith that draws us into a relationship with God? 'Now by this we know that we know Him, if we keep His commandments. He who says, 'I know Him,' and does not keep His commandments, is a liar and the truth is not in him' (1 John 2:3–4). Faith without works is dead.

The proper combination of faith and obedience can be summed up in one word: holiness. Holiness means being so full of God that there is no room for anything else. That means that we no longer love the world or the things of the world such as the lust of the flesh, the lust of the eyes and the pride of life. Instead of doing the things of the world, a holy person does the will of God. All this is in 1 John 2, where it is summed up in the context of spiritual warfare: 'You are strong and the word of God abides in you, and you have overcome the wicked one' (1 John 2:14).

If we pray with an attitude of faith and obedience, the specific weapons which God has given us for spiritual warfare will be effective in defeating the enemy. What are some of these specific weapons?

The Name of Jesus

There are several biblical references which point to the importance of Jesus' name. Mark quotes Jesus as saying that we cast out demons in Jesus' name (Mk. 16:17). John quotes Jesus as saying, 'If you ask anything in My name I will do it' (Jn. 14:14). Paul says that God gave Jesus the name which is above every name (Phil. 2:9), just to mention a few examples.

What's so important about a name? It is the authority that the name bears. An American ambassador to a foreign country speaks in the name of the President of the United States. A police officer knocks on a door and says, 'Open up in the name of the law!' The other day I answered the telephone and a voice said, 'I'm Susan and I'm calling Doris Wagner for Pat Robertson.' I immediately summoned my wife Doris to the phone only to discover the call was an appeal for funds. My habit is to hang up on such telemarketers, but the name 'Pat Robertson' hooked me. And Susan got $100 from Doris! The name carries authority.

When Jesus invites us to use His name, He transfers divine authority. It is an awesome weapon, but caution is needed. In Acts 19 we are told of the seven sons of Sceva who tried to cast out a demon in Jesus' name only to find out that the spirit knew they were phonies and called their bluff. The one demonized man beat up all seven, stripped them naked and chased them out of the house. No one has the authority of Jesus unless Jesus is truly their Lord. At the judgment many will say, 'Lord, have we not prophesied in Your name?' and Jesus will reply, 'I never knew you' (Mt. 7:22–23).

The name of Jesus is a powerful weapon of spiritual warfare and it wields tremendous authority, but only if we use it according to His will.

The Blood of Jesus

Revelation 12 relates one of the fiercest episodes of spiritual warfare imaginable. Michael and his angels are fighting against the dragon and his angels. Michael wins 'by the blood of the Lamb' (Rev. 12:11).

When Jesus shed His blood on the cross, Satan's power was definitively broken. It was on the cross that Jesus 'disarmed principalities and powers' and 'made a public spectacle of them' (Col. 2:14–15). Satan hates nothing more than to be reminded of the blood of Jesus. The cross is an embarrassment to him. Every soul saved by the blood of Jesus is a further embarrassment to him. Satan cannot stand his ground against the blood of Jesus.

I teach the 120 Fellowship adult Sunday School class in Lake Avenue Congregational Church in Pasadena, California. This is a Third Wave class in which we have experienced the miraculous power of God for several years. Although we have ministered to the demonized through the years, we were spared from open demonic manifestations in class until I began a six-month series on spiritual warfare, teaching many of the concepts found in this chapter. During that time we experienced two powerful manifestations.

In one of the instances I had bound the demons before they had made any noise and was gathering a small team to minister to the woman. One of the team members somewhat routinely claimed the power of the blood of Jesus Christ. Just the mention of the blood totally changed the situation from relative quiet into shrieks and screams 'NOT THE BLOOD! NOT THE BLOOD!' While claiming and applying the blood of Christ must not be regarded as some magic formula, it certainly must be recognized as a powerful weapon of spiritual warfare.

Agreement

Undoubtedly the greatest day in the history of the church was the day of Pentecost. On that day 'they were all with one accord' (Acts 2:1). The accord was 'in prayer and supplication' (Acts 1:14). Few weapons of spiritual warfare are more effective than agreement in prayer.

What is it we agree upon? We agree first of all on what the Word of God is saying to us. Then we agree on what we see the Father doing by the Holy Spirit. Even Jesus said He did only what He saw the Father doing (see Jn. 5:19). It is possible for us to know individually what the Father is doing, but given our human tendency toward the world and the flesh we are on much safer ground when others agree with us.

Jesus sums it up when He says, 'If two of you agree on earth concerning anything that they ask, it will be done for them by My Father in heaven' (Mt. 18:19). This is one reason why corporate prayer is so important in spiritual warfare. When numbers of believers in one local church or from many churches in the same area get together to agree in prayer, power against the enemy increases dramatically.

Fasting

While there may be several forms of fasting, at this point I am referring to voluntarily abstaining from food for a given period of time. This is the most common sense of the term.

Apparently some forms of spiritual warfare require fasting as a prerequisite for victory. When Jesus was explaining to His disciples why they couldn't cast the demon out of the epileptic boy, He said, 'This kind does not go out except by prayer and fasting' (Mt. 17:21).

The apostles fasted when they wanted to hear from God. When the prophets and teachers in Antioch fasted, the Holy Spirit spoke and told them to send out Barnabas and Saul. Then they fasted again before they laid on hands and sent them out (see Acts 13:2–3).

The highest level power encounter of all time was Jesus' temptation in the wilderness. As a part of it, Jesus fasted for 40 days. Did that weaken Him? Yes, it weakened Him physically, but it strengthened Him spiritually. Paul says, 'When I am weak, then I am strong (2 Cor. 12:10).

We must be careful that we take the proper attitude toward fasting. Fasting is a privilege which draws us closer to God and makes us more sensitive to hearing from Him. It is not a spiritual merit badge which makes us better than others. It is not a method of manipulating God into doing what we want Him to do. Jesus says that we are not supposed to make a public display of fasting, but to do it quietly to the Father (see Mt. 6:16–18). This does not mean we shouldn't talk about it discreetly, but it does mean we shouldn't brag about it.

With the right attitude and with God's timing and guidance, fasting is one of our most useful weapons.

Praise

We often think of praise only as an expression of joy when something good happens to us. We hear of some victory and say, almost as a reflex action, 'Praise the Lord!' But there is more to praise than that. Our praise, under any circumstances, blesses God. The psalmist says, 'Every day I will bless You and I will praise Your name forever and ever' (Ps. 145:2).

Paul and Silas show us clearly how powerful praise can be as a weapon of spiritual warfare. In Philippi Paul had cast a high-ranking spirit of divination out of a fortune teller. Her masters were incensed and had Paul and Silas beaten and thrown into jail. They found themselves in the inner prison with their feet in stocks. One could hardly imagine a more dismal and discouraging situation.

What did Paul and Silas do? They praised God! 'At midnight Paul and Silas were praying and singing hymns to God' (Acts 16:25). The result was a divine earthquake which loosened their chains and opened the prison doors. The jailer himself was saved and a strong church was planted. Paul and Silas were victorious, but the secret was that they had praised God even before they saw the victory.

The Word of God

In Ephesians 6 the full armor of God is described in detail. Of the six pieces of armor, five are defensive weapons and only one offensive – the sword of the Spirit which is the word of God (Eph. 6:17).

What is the word of God?

The use of the written word of God, the scriptures, is a powerful weapon of warfare as we see in the temptation of Jesus. As a response to all three attacks of the devil, Jesus quoted Old Testament scriptures and the devil could not resist.

But there is also a spoken word of God, a *rhema*, which I will explain in more detail later one. At this point I simply want to indicate that hearing a fresh, spoken word of God is an important part of using the sword of the Spirit.

An example from the Old Testament is found in Jeremiah 32. Jeremiah said, 'The word of the Lord came to me' (Jer. 32:6). This word happened to refer to a man named Hanamel who would approach him and ask him to buy a field. When it came true, Jeremiah said, 'Then I knew that this was the word of the Lord' (Jer. 32:8).

The sword of the Spirit is hearing from God like Jeremiah did. It is knowing what God's will is for a certain time and place. It is following in the steps of Jesus who said, 'The Son can do nothing of Himself, but what He sees the Father do' (Jn. 5:19).

This is why prayer is part of the same sentence (even though some editions of the Bible separate Ephesians 6:18 from 6:17 by a subtitle) that mentions the sword of the Spirit. It is only by 'praying always with all prayer and supplication in the Spirit' (Eph. 6:18) that we are in a position to receive the word of God. True prayer is a two-way conversation with God. We speak to Him and He speaks to us.

Knowing God's will by receiving the word of God and acting accordingly is crucial to effective spiritual warfare. Fasting is related to this since it makes our spiritual ears more sensitive, and agreement with other believers helps protect us when we are not hearing as accurately as we should. When accurately discerned, the word of God is an extremely powerful weapon.

The weapons of our warfare are spiritual, not carnal. As we mature in the things of God we will better learn how to use the name of Jesus, the blood of Jesus, agreement, fasting, praise and the word of God. These are not the only weapons we have for spiritual warfare we have, but they are extremely important in resisting the enemy.

2. Our Spiritual Authority

Once we understand our spiritual weapons and something of how to use them, we then need to focus our attention on the divine authority which forms the basis on which we operate. One of the weapons, the name of Jesus, gives us a clue to the nature of our authority. It is in the name of Jesus that we are authorized to bind and loose. What does this mean?

Jesus spoke of binding and loosing at Caesarea Philippi in what is widely regarded as one of the milestone events of His training of the twelve apostles. The incident is described in Matthew 16, and Jesus makes three important points:

1. **The Messiah has come**. Simon Peter confesses, on behalf of all, that 'You are the Christ, the Son of the living God' (Mt. 16:16). They know the world will never be the same again. The one for whom the Jews had been waiting thousands of years was there in their midst.

2. **The church has come**. The twelve were now ready to hear: 'On this rock I will build My church' (Mt. 16:18). It was Jesus' intention that the church would advance, and He assured them that even 'the gates of Hades shall not prevail against it' (Mt. 16:18).

3. **The kingdom has come**. Jesus promises His followers the keys of the kingdom of heaven. What are they? He says, 'Whatever you bind on earth will be bound in heaven, and whatever you loose on earth will be loosed in heaven' (Mt. 16:19).

Binding and Loosing

A little later on, Jesus repeats His teaching on binding and loosing, and adds, 'Where two or three are gathered together in

My name, there I am in the midst of them' (Mt. 18:20). This seems to be a delegated authority which common believers would be expected to use today.

'Binding' (Greek *deo*) is frequently used for tying up an animal. For example, a watchdog will keep one away from its master's house unless it is bound. Likewise, Jesus says, 'How can one enter a strong man's house and plunder his goods, unless he first *binds* the strong man?' (Mt. 12:29). In the context of spiritual warfare, binding means restricting the power of evil on all levels.

'Loosing' (Greek *luo*) often means untying the thong on sandals. Jesus said concerning Lazarus, 'Loose him and let him go.' He also declared that a woman whom Satan had bound for eighteen years 'ought to be *loosed* from this bond' (Luke 13:16).

It is important to realize that while we have authority to bind and loose in the name of Jesus, we do not decide on our own what should be bound and what should be loosed. The Greek tense of Jesus' teaching really means: what you bind on earth *will have been* bound in heaven and what you loose on earth *will have been* loosed in heaven. This indicates the necessity for a synchronization between earth and heaven. The normal sequence is heaven first, then earth. This once again reminds us of the need to hear from God in prayer and know what He is doing before undertaking any aspect of spiritual warfare.

How do we know what God is doing in heaven?

While the difference cannot be pressed to an extreme because there is some overlapping of terms, some Pentecostal theologians have made the helpful suggestion of distinguishing the *logos* word of God from the *rhema* word of God. The *logos* is said to be God's eternal, written word found in the canon of scripture. Through it we know, for example, that sin has been bound in heaven. So, more specifically, have lust and pride and bitterness, to name just a few. So have demons. We need look no further to know that we have the authority to bind the spiritual forces behind war or oppression or child abuse or racism or pornography because God's written word gives us that information.

The *rhema* is regarded as a more immediate word from God which we do not find in the 66 books of the Bible. Although it will never contradict the written word of God, it is something we seek directly from the Father. For example, we want to buy a home and we pray, 'God, is this the one?' Or we look for a job and pray, 'God, please show me if it is your will that I accept this offer.' We pray believing that He will give us the answer. What are commonly (though questionably) referred to as 'words of knowledge' also fall into the *rhema* category.

A while ago, for instance, a woman in my 120 Fellowship adult Sunday School class announced that God had spoken a *rhema* word to her that someone in the class was suffering from a severe affliction of the lower intestine which God wanted us to pray for. When no one responded, she was surprised because she thought she had received the word quite clearly, including several details of what the affliction actually looked like. During the week as she prayed further about it she received another word from God, this time the actual first and last name of the gentleman who was sick. That brother had been absent from the class the Sunday she spoke up, but when he came the following Sunday there was no doubt about whether we had the authority to bind the affliction because we knew it had been bound in heaven. We prayed for him and he was healed. In this case our instructions had to come through a *rhema* word rather than a *logos* word.

How do we know if a *rhema* word is valid? How do we know that what we are hearing is not just our own imagination or, worse, something generated by the world, the flesh or the devil?

Spiritual gifts, such as the gift of prophecy or the gift of discernment of spirits come into the picture at this point. They are extremely helpful. So are experience and Christian maturity and holiness and personal intimacy with God. These go a long way in providing assurance to an individual such as the woman who had the word about the intestinal disease.

But there is an even greater assurance when the word is allowed to be tested by others. I believe this is why Jesus directly followed His teaching on binding and loosing by saying that He is present when two or three are gathered together in His name. 'If two of you agree on earth concerning anything they ask, it will be done for them by My Father who is in heaven' (Mt. 18:19). One of the things we need to agree on is discerning what has been bound in heaven.

One of the most serious crises in the history of my 120 Fellowship Sunday School class arose when we had invited a woman to give us some of our first teaching on contemporary prophecy. The enemy obviously did not want this to happen and he confused us enough to make some class leaders think that it was not God's will. I myself had no *rhema* word on this one, so I called my leadership team together for an emergency meeting. Although we did not agree with each other when we started the meeting, before long we collectively discerned that God wanted us to go ahead with our plans. I was in a personal position where I could not have known this alone. But once we agreed that we had a word from God we bound the enemy and loosed the ministry of the woman we had invited. Not surprisingly, the event turned out to be a powerful landmark occasion for the group as a whole as well as for numerous individuals and families.

It Doesn't Always Work!

Almost any of us who can tell stories like the two I have told above can tell even more stories in which binding and loosing have not accomplished the desired results. Why is this?

There must be many reasons, and I do not profess to know them all. It does seem to me, however, that there may be both external and internal reasons for failure.

Externally, it is very simple. Satan obstructs the process. We are told that he 'walks about like a roaring lion, seeking whom he may devour' (1 Peter 5:8). Obviously he is not omnipresent, so he obstructs us from accurately discerning the will of God through demons of different ranks. The higher the rank of the evil spirit, the more spiritual power is needed to bind it. Unfortunately many who shout in churches or in rallies on television, 'I bind you, Satan!' are operating on such a low level of spiritual power that they are not accomplishing much more than making noise. While we are assured that Satan is ultimately defeated, we run a great risk when we underestimate his cunningness and power. Nevertheless, when we find that we are impotent in binding and loosing, we do well to search for a possible cause in the spirit world.

Internally, it is quite possible that those of us who are attempting to do spiritual warfare are not properly submitted to the lordship of Christ. His authority and power flow through us only when we maintain an intimate relationship with Him. To the degree that we are not living holy lives we can expect a reduction in spiritual power. It is all too easy for any of us to revert to using carnal, rather than spiritual, weapons in our lives and ministries. When we do, binding and loosing has little effect.

3. Our Engagement with the Enemy

Having understood the weapons of our warfare and our authority to use them, we are ready to consider moving out and engaging the enemy.

As spiritual warfare rises toward the top of the agendas of Christian leaders in many parts of the world, it is to be expected that a variety of opinions will emerge. The discussion as to just how directly we should engage the enemy is an extremely important one. Some come at it with a more cautious approach while others seem to be considerably bolder. I say it is important because we are dealing here with what can escalate into a life and death issue.

The more cautious souls have frequently come to their position because of disastrous events they themselves have experienced or that they have heard of. Underestimating the power of the enemy is a major danger, and some have paid the price for falling into it. I know of several American pastors who have taken on territorial spirits and ended up leaving the ministry because of immorality. A Japanese pastor told me of a church member who brought a family idol to be destroyed, but also said he had been warned that if it was destroyed someone in his family would die. He burned the idol in the patio of the church, and within six months a cousin's son died and his wife lost her first child. A Presbyterian pastor in Ghana ordered a tree which had become a satanic shrine to be cut down. When the last branch was lopped off, the pastor dropped dead.

Stories like this are frightening. Who would not be cautious if they knew that not only their own physical life and well-being were at stake, but also those of their loved ones? Some see their role as that of Daniel in the story of the great heavenly battle which took place between angels and the princes of Persia and Greece described in Daniel 10. Daniel did not engage the enemy directly. In fact, he apparently did not even know a battle was taking place. He stayed home and prayed to God, yet his prayer triggered the cosmic struggle. Even Michael the archangel at one time did not dare to accuse the devil, but asked the Lord to do it for him (see Jude 9).

Appropriate caution, then, is called for in all spiritual warfare. At the same time, however, there seems to be a concomitant biblical mandate for boldness in engaging the enemy. Some particular challenges by the enemy require that, if we are wise, we will edge toward the side of caution. Other challenges will require us to be somewhat more aggressive. If we are hearing the voice of God, as we should be, we will take our cues from Him and move out accordingly.

Returning to Ephesians 6, we see that our engagement with the enemy is described in some detail, with the Apostle Paul characteristically mixing metaphors. He uses two simultaneous analogies to describe our engagement with the enemy: the wrestler and the warrior.

The Wrestler

Paul says that 'we do not wrestle against flesh and blood, but against principalities, against powers, against the rulers of the darkness of this age, against spiritual hosts of wickedness in the heavenly places' (Eph. 6:12). In the Graeco-Roman culture, wrestling was a prominent sport. Wrestling, even more than, say, boxing or karate, requires a high degree of direct bodily contact with the opponent. The goal of the wrestler was not to protect himself, although that was an important means to an end. His goal was to conquer the opponent in physical engagement. The winner came out on top and the loser came out on the bottom. In fact, some Greek wrestling involved a fight to the death.

Paul is speaking about very serious spiritual business. When he says that 'we' wrestle, he is not referring just to himself, Silas and Timothy. He is referring to all true members of the body of Christ. He does not suggest that we wrestle directly with the devil because for one thing the devil, as I have mentioned previously, cannot be in more than one place at one time. The principalities, powers, rulers of darkness, and spiritual hosts of wickedness are descriptions of the demonic hordes whom Satan has delegated to steal, to kill and to destroy, and those are the beings whom we are expected to engage.

In most cases we will be called to wrestle against ground-level spirits such as those frequently mentioned in the Gospels. Some may also be called to deal with the middle-level spirits which operate through witches, occult practitioners, New Age channelers, spiritist mediums and others. Paul dealt with one of these in Philippi, a spirit of divination which had controlled a slave girl who was a fortune teller. This was such a high-level spirit that the deliverance had political repercussions and Paul and Silas found themselves in jail as a result (see Acts 16:16–24). Others, I would think relatively few, may be called to deal with the higher level territorial spirits such as the Prince of Persia or the Prince of Greece. Obviously, the higher we go the more caution we need.

The Warrior

Once he establishes that our engagement with wicked spirits is like a wrestler, Paul switches analogies and describes our means of combat as that of a Roman warrior.

Military equipment, then as now, includes defensive as well as offensive instruments. The full armor of God is our defense against our spiritual enemies. Interestingly enough, the Roman armor was designed to protect the front of the warrior, not the back. Apparently the assumption was that when the enemies were near, the soldiers were moving toward them, not running away. But as any soldier knows, the final objective is not to protect yourself against the enemies, but to defeat them. General Patton once said the key to winning a war is not giving your life for your country, but seeing that the enemy gives his life for his country.

Paul mentions two offensive weapons in this passage, one used by the devil and one used by the Christian warrior. The devil's weapon is a bow and arrow (Eph. 6:16). This is a weapon used at a distance. It may well be Satan's desire that his forces do not engage well-armed Christians up close. On the other hand, the Christian's weapon is a sword, a close-up weapon. Satan may continue shooting from a distance and we are expected to use the shield of faith to defend ourselves. But if we are going to use our sword we must be prepared to engage the enemy.

4. Our Plan of Action

There is no doubt about it. Engaging the enemy on any level is risky business. Nor is there any doubt that we are called to do it. So now the question becomes, how do we go about it? If we are going to do spiritual warfare, let us do it well. Let us agree on a wise and effective plan of action.

One of the most helpful scripture passages for formulating a battle plan is James 4:7–8: 'Therefore submit to God. Resist the devil and he will flee from you. Draw near to God and He will draw near to you. Cleanse your hands, you sinners; and purify your hearts, you double-minded.'

This passage mentions two relationships with seven verbs, five of them active and two passive. The first relationship is upward and the second is outward.

The Upward Relationship – God
Four active verbs are used to describe our relationship to God: submit, draw near, cleanse, and purify.

21

First, we are to submit to God. This means, first and fore-most, to accept Jesus Christ as Savior, and acknowledge that He is Lord. As we do, we enter the family of God. God is our Father. It is a comfortable situation for us to be at home on our Father's lap, so to speak.

Secondly, we are to draw near to God. This means we must spend time with the Father. We must get to know Him well, and as in any other interpersonal relationship, time together is of the essence. One of the obvious reasons we need to be near to God is to know from Him what has already been bound in heaven so we can effectively bind on earth.

Then, we are to cleanse our hands and purify our hearts. Cleansing our hands refers to what we do. Purifying our hearts refers to our motives, what we think and feel. Taken together they point us toward holiness. Holiness, as I understand it, is being so full of God that there is no room for anything else. Without holiness we can expect very little power in spiritual warfare. The opposite of holiness is worldliness, and a previous verse in James 4 reminds us that 'friendship with the world is enmity with God' (Jas. 4:4). While we no more produce personal holiness through human works than we gain salvation through them, if we decide to open our lives totally to the fullness of the Holy Spirit, He is the one who does the work of cleansing and purifying.

If we take the action, then, of submitting, drawing near, cleansing and purifying, the passive verb comes into play: 'God will draw near to you.' This is God's action, not ours.

When He draws near to us, our chief desire is to obey Him. We want to please the one who loves us so much. In describing the weapons of our warfare in 2 Corinthians 10, Paul says they are to 'bring every thought into captivity to the *obedience* of Christ' (2 Cor. 10:5).

The Outward Relationship – Satan

While our first movement in spiritual warfare is upward toward God, our second is outward toward the enemy. Here we have only one active verb: resist. If we take steps to resist the devil, the passive verb comes into play and 'he will flee from you.'

22

This is the scary part. Nothing scares a little bird more than being pushed out of the nest. Nothing scares us more than the thought of meeting the enemy in a spiritual wrestling match. Satan is a roaring lion. Who wants to go in that direction? It would be much more comfortable to run back home to Mommie. But the verb is not 'run away' or 'stay out of the jungle' or 'ignore him,' but **resist**. We may not like the idea, but we must move in the outward direction.

Jesus Himself had to go through a similar process. From all of eternity He had been equal to the Father. But, as Philippians 2 teaches us, He became unequal to the Father by taking on a human nature in the incarnation. Jesus had to come to earth, live a human life, experience temptation just as we do, and resist the devil one-on-one, not as God but as a human being. I would imagine that doing that was as scary for Him as spiritual warfare is for us. He knows by personal experience what He is sending us out to do.

The twelve apostles had been with Jesus for a year and a half. They had grown to love Him and to love each other. But the day finally came when they were to minister on their own. Jesus told them that the harvest was ready and that they were to go out by themselves to reap it by preaching the kingdom of God and manifesting the signs of the kingdom. After a year and a half of moving upward, so to speak, they now were to move outward. This was scary, especially when Jesus said, 'Behold, I send you out as sheep in the midst of wolves' (Matt. 10:16). But they obeyed, and much to their relief they did have the power to cast out demons and heal the sick (Mark 6:13).

Later Jesus sent seventy of His followers out, giving them 'authority to trample on serpents and scorpions, and over all the power of the enemy' (Luke 10:19). Their ministry was so powerful that Jesus 'saw Satan fall from heaven like lightning' (Luke 10:18) as they were preaching and doing good works.

The apostles as well as the seventy had submitted to God and God had drawn near to them. Then they resisted the devil and he indeed fled from them as the scripture says he will.

Finding the Balance

As we today begin to learn how to move out in spiritual warfare on all levels as did the early Christians, it is essential that we maintain the delicate balance between the upward and the outward. I like to conceptualize it in a diagram such as the following:

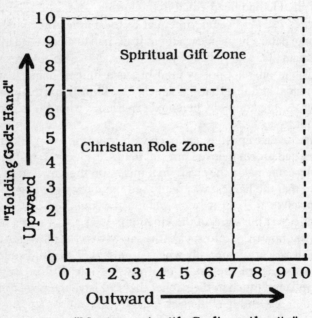

Positions in Spiritual Warfare:
The Upward and the Outward

How does this model function? It is simple. We must never move outward faster than we move upward. The upward is an indispensable prerequisite for the outward, since nothing we do is derived from our own strength, but rather from the strength provided by God through us.

What happens if we are out of balance?

The danger of going upward without going outward is ineffectiveness in ministry. This is serious enough.

But the danger of going outward without going upward is much more serious. It is truly like being a sheep among wolves, but this time a sheep without the protection of the Great Shepherd. The enemy can and will eat us for breakfast.

How far out should we go? Those who have read my book *Your Spiritual Gifts Can Help Your Church Grow* may recall the helpful distinction between spiritual gifts and Christian roles. It is a Christian role for every believer to engage in ministries such as evangelism, giving, hospitality, healing, teaching and any number of others as needs and opportunities arise. But this is not to deny that God has also given to a certain number of members of the body of Christ special spiritual gifts known, for example, as the gift of evangelist or the gift of healing or the gift of teaching, in which case the ministry of those individuals will be done on a much broader, more systematic and more effective scale than that of the average Christian.

This applies to spiritual warfare. I know of no 'gift of spiritual warfare' in the New Testament, but I do believe that some Christians have been given a gift mix through which God expects them to move outward more than others. I have arbitrarily numbered the vertical and horizontal scales of the model from 0 to 10 and drawn internal boundaries with the dotted line at 7 on the upward scale and 7 on the outward scale. It simply indicates that there is probably some limit to the level of spiritual warfare which the ordinary Christian without a special gift mix or ministry or calling should reasonably undertake. Past that, especially when it involves dealing with territorial spirits such as are described in this book, only those so gifted and called would be advised to attempt it. Few would be expected to be doing level 8 spiritual warfare, and fewer still level 9. The only human being who would legitimately be a 10–10 on the scale would be Jesus Christ, and His face-to-face encounter with Satan in the wilderness might well be regarded as a unique experience which will not be duplicated.

Since it is advisable to be further up than out at any given time, I like to go one step further and superimpose over the diagram a 'danger zone' in which we should avoid ministering at all costs. In other words, never allow yourself to be found ministering in a position within the shaded zone:

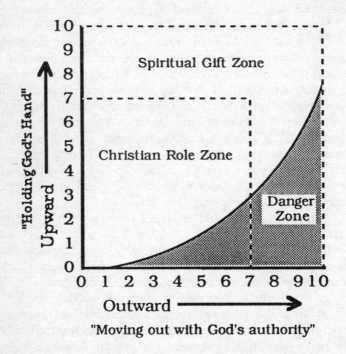

Keep in mind that these lines are arbitrary and illustrative only. Perhaps as time goes by and we experiment more with spiritual warfare we will be able to draw some more objective conclusions.

Meanwhile as we strive to hear from God and to know the level and intensity on which He might be calling each of us to engage in spiritual warfare, we can be sure that as we move upward God will draw near to us and as we appropriately move outward Satan will flee from us. The scriptures promise us that. And as the power of the enemy is pushed back and the glory of God shines through, we will see the harvest increasingly reaped and multitudes of unbelievers turning 'from darkness to light, and from the power of Satan to God' (Acts 26:18).

2

Defeating Territorial Spirits

by Steven Lawson

It will be useful, near the beginning of a volume of this nature to see, with rather broad brush strokes, a panorama of some of the new things the Spirit is apparently saying to the churches. Steven Lawson is a journalist on the staff of Charisma & Christian Life *magazine, a principal voice of the Pentecostal/charismatic movement in the United States. This article, written specifically to communicate to Christian laypeople, appeared as a feature cover story in the April 1990 issue of that magazine. Its lively style gives us a glimpse of the thoughts of some of the leading Christian figures in the U.S.A., and furnishes a backdrop against which to interpret some of the chapters which follow.*

* * * * *

Cordoba, Argentina. Two hundred Youth With a Mission (YWAM) missionaries are frustrated, discouraged. They have come from around the world to tell fans

---

attending the 1978 world soccer finals about Jesus. But no one seems to be listening to their good news. Their evangelism efforts become listless, powerless; their Spanish-language gospel tracts ignored, tossed aside.

Not quick to give up, the YWAM missionaries declare a day of fasting and prayer, and retreat to a monastery on the edge of town. There they engage in spiritual warfare.

God makes them aware of the true nature of the battle they are fighting. It goes beyond demons attacking individuals. God shows how Satan has immersed himself in the culture of the area. He reveals a demonic principality that reigns in Cordoba: Pride.

Very sophisticated, fashion-conscious and materialistic, Cordoba's residents cling to values of position, possessions and appearance. The spirit of pride that manifests itself in these ways can be overcome in only one way – through humility.

Scattering themselves throughout the central mall shopping area, YWAM team members fall to their knees. With their foreheads to the cobblestones, in full view of passers-by, they pray for a revelation of Jesus to the city.

A breakthrough comes immediately. Large, curious crowds gather to watch and listen. Men, women and children ask the missionaries to autograph the tracts they now take gladly. As outreach leader John Dawson preaches at the Plaza of St. Martin, people in the crowd drop to their knees, repenting of their sins. In a flood of tears, one woman asks Dawson if she can accept Christ as her Savior right there or if she has to go to church to do it.

'The intimidation of the enemy was broken along with our pride,' says Dawson, now the ministry's Southwest United States director.

What Dawson and his fellow YWAM missionaries participated in was full-scale spiritual warfare. What they accomplished was the breaking of a spiritual stronghold. From Cordoba, Argentina, to San Jose, California, to Sofia, Bulgaria, the supernatural battle rages, with Christians responding like never before.

What once was limited to intercessory prayer and an occasional deliverance from demonic possession is now unfolding as a major aspect of church life. Dawson employs the principles regularly in his work with Youth With a Mission in Southern California. Larry Lea, pastor of Church on the Rock, Rockwall, Texas, has called an army of prayer warriors to 'do battle with the enemy.' Earl Paulk of Chapel Hill Harvester in Atlanta, Georgia, has said that as we enter the 1990s we embark upon the most intense time of spiritual warfare in history.

But the struggle is not new at all. The apostle Paul tells us that this battle we fight is not 'against flesh and blood.' Rather, we struggle 'against the rulers, against the authorities, against the powers of this dark world and against the spiritual forces of evil in heavenly realms' (Eph. 6:12, NIV).

With his novels *This Present Darkness* and *Piercing the Darkness*, Frank Peretti has popularized the conflict that Paul was describing. These fictionalized accounts tell how packs of demons have taken over complete towns, infesting government, education, even churches. And they depict how Christians fight back with prayer and how angels clash with evil principalities.

More and more people such as Dawson, Lea and Paulk are taking Paul's words seriously and applying as fact the same principles Peretti used to craft his novels.

We live in the midst of a real-life, invisible, spiritual war, says Dawson. The combatants include angels, demons, Satan, the Holy Spirit and us. The battlefronts can be found at every point on the globe. The stakes are the salvation of human beings.

Evanston, Illinois. Steve Nicholson has preached the gospel in the area for six years, with virtually no fruit. He and members of his church pray for the sick and a few get well. But his Vineyard Christian Fellowship is not growing. Nicholson begins some serious prayer and fasting.

31

A grotesque, unnatural being appears to him. It growls, 'Why are you bothering me?' It identifies itself as a demon of witchcraft who has dominion over the geographical area.

In the heat of warfare, Nicholson names the city streets in the surrounding area. The spirit retorts, 'I don't want to give you that much.' In the name of Jesus, Nicholson commands the spirit to give up the territory.

During the next three months the church doubles in size from 70 to 150, mostly from new converts coming out of witchcraft. Nearly all of the new believers must be delivered from demons.

For the most part, dealing directly with the demonic has been limited to possession or oppression of individuals. While this remains a vital part of the battle, a new front has emerged: territorial spirits, such as the spirit of pride and the spirit of witchcraft.

Professor C. Peter Wagner of Fuller Theological Seminary's School of World Mission calls this 'cosmic-level' warfare and identifies different tiers of demonic activity, even a hierarchy. Dawson, Lea and others say specific principalities with identifiable characteristics are assigned to specific geographical locations and geopolitical institutions. Their domain can include a household, a neighborhood, a city, a nation, a culture, a subculture.

The dominating characteristic of these spirits can be greed (New York City), power (Washington, D.C.), pornography (Los Angeles), lust, timidity, pride or other sin. Lea says the spirit of greed seems to dominate many areas of the United States.

Orlando, Florida. Cars barely crawl along South Orange Blossom Trail on this Friday night. Commuters head home; tourists wind their way to their hotels; men try to go unnoticed as they enter the topless bars that line the street.

Jim Gaines, a balding, 50-year-old church elder, pulls his car into a parking space across the street from an adult bookstore. He shuts off the headlights, turns off the engine and quotes 2 Corinthians 10:4: 'For the weapons of our warfare are not carnal, but mighty through God to the pulling down of strongholds.' Ann Agee and Norma Gray, who have come with Gaines on this night, nod in agreement. For the next 30 minutes or so the three praise God and rebuke the devil – as they and others have on several nights a month for several months.

'We bind the spirit of lust and sexual perversion in this place,' Agee commands. 'We marshal angels to take charge and to speak to the hearts of the men who enter this building,' Gray declares. 'We take authority in the name of Jesus,' Gaines exclaims.

Two weeks later and a half-mile down the road at a combined meeting of several Orlando churches, Metro Life Church pastor Danny Jones leads about 500 Christians in prayer for the city. Then they enter into spiritual warfare, denouncing the demonic spirits that blind the eyes of non-Christians in the city and pulling down the strongholds that rule over the region. Specifically they denounce the spirits that control the 'adult entertainment' businesses that sell pornography.

Within a month, the city's Metropolitan Bureau of Investigation has enough evidence to start legal proceedings that could close the adult bookstores. Within two months, owners of all seven adult bookstores in the greater Orlando area voluntarily shut their doors.

John Dawson has just published a book titled *Taking Our Cities for God: How to Break Spiritual Strongholds* (Creation House). In the book he expands upon his teachings on territorial spirits. C. Peter Wagner calls this the most important book on the subject and the only textbook available. Jack Hayford, pastor of The Church On the Way in Van Nuys, California, wrote in the foreword: 'This is a book of Holy Spirit insight. It juxtaposes the inspired Word of God with the toughest problems we face on this planet today and shows how timeless truth relates to and can transform our present entanglements.'

Dawson uses his Cordoba experience as a launching pad into his broadened understanding of the theology of intercession for our cities. This intercession involves warfare. Dawson carefully charts a course that includes personal holiness, discerning of spirits, praise and worship, prayer, research, obedience to God, unity and direct confrontation.

Dawson, now 38, grew up in New Zealand, the oldest child of Jim and Joy Dawson and the grandson of a Plymouth Brethren radio evangelist. Loren Cunningham, YWAM international director, describes Jim and Joy Dawson's household as being one of the most spiritual he has ever seen. 'They had a constant flow of prayer and Bible study,' says Cunningham. Evangelist Steve Fry, who knew Dawson when they were both teenagers, remembers Dawson as being sensitive to the Holy Spirit and one desiring, even at a young age, an intimate relationship with God.

After graduating from high school, Dawson was in Switzerland, attending a YWAM training school. There was no doubt in Dawson's mind that God had called him to be a missionary. The big question was where: Germany, the jungles of New Guinea, the rain forests of the Amazon? All seemed reasonable.

Finally, he spent an entire day in prayer, asking God to show him to which nation He was sending him. He promised God that wherever it was, he would serve there the remainder of his life.

The next morning Dawson awoke with a Bible reference fixed in his mind: Ezekiel 3:5. He had never read Ezekiel, so he had no idea that the verse said, 'You are not sent to a people of unfamiliar speech and of a hard language, but to the house of Israel' (NKJV). Before that day was out, God made it clear that He was calling Dawson to the United States of America. Though not his native nation, his parents had moved to Southern California several years earlier.

Memphis, Tennessee. Contemporary Christian singer Keith Green has taken John Dawson along on a concert tour. They discern spirits of apathy and religion in the city and confront them. That night, they turn the concert into a giant worship service. Green turns off all the lights during the concert and preaches on commitment to God and repentance from dead works. There is neither space nor a dry eye at the altar.

Green's widow, Melody, says the concept of spiritual battle in a given city before and during a concert transformed his singing ministry in his last days. She says that Dawson and Green became close friends and that Dawson has since shared this and other teachings with the Garden Valley Christian Artist retreat, which is held each year in Lindale, Texas.

Fuller Seminary professor C. Peter Wagner explains that Satan is not like God. He cannot be omnipresent. He was created as an angel, but chose to turn from God and took one-third of the angels with him. These fallen angels became demons.

In his book *Angels: God's Secret Agents*, Billy Graham says that the fallen angels chose to participate in 'the war program of Lucifer.' The object of their program, according to Graham, is to destroy faith in the world. Satan and his evil spirits want to perpetuate unbelief and keep the gospel from being preached, affirms Wagner.

Since Satan, the fallen prince of heaven, cannot be omnipresent, he must delegate the responsibility of evil influence to his demonic servants. How many demons are there? Wagner reports that though no exact count can be arrived at, some hints have been given:

Wagner tells of Friday Thomas Ajah – a Sunday school superintendent at the Assembles of God church in Oribe, Port Harcourt, Nigeria – who was a high-ranking occult leader before his conversion. Ajah was purportedly given the name of St. Thomas the Divine by Satan, He reports that Satan had assigned him control of 12 spirits and that each spirit controlled 600 demons for a total of 7,212.

'I was in touch with all the spirits controlling each town in Nigeria, and I had a shrine in all the major cities,' Ajah says.

The nature of demons can be argued. Some theologians such as Wagner contend that these spirits can attach themselves to people, buildings, seats of government and other objects. Others offer a more vague description, contending that since demons also battle in the heavenlies they have attributes humans cannot comprehend just as angels cannot be fully understood.

San José, California. Pastor Dick Bernal, members of his Jubilee Christian Center and Christians from a number of other churches plan to 'attack the city' in intercessory prayer. Some rent rooms on the top floor of hotels; others assemble on a nearby hill; still others gain access to the rooftops of tall buildings.

Through research, they had traced the history of the area back to the 19th-century California Gold Rush. Bernal says that the type of people attracted by instant riches produced the spirit of greed that now manifests itself in the materialistic norms of the business community in Silicon Valley, which San Jose anchors, and the self-centered experimental lifestyle of the entire San Francisco area.

Concerned that the San Francisco-San Jose-Oakland area sits alone as the only major metropolis in the United States never to experience a major revival, they began to pray. Quickly the principality of 'self' was identified as dominant.

The Christians gathered around the high places of San Jose start with praise and worship, then prayer, and then they confront the spirits. Specifically, they declare that the skies of their city will be opened and the light of the gospel will get through to the unsaved.

Dawson encourages the research of local history before entering spiritual warfare or serious intercession for a city. In Annapolis, Maryland, a spirit of 'bondage' is traced back to the slave trade that was conducted there. In Nashville, Tennessee, the spirit of 'religiosity' finds its roots in the institutionalized but inactive church denominations that have had a strong presence there. In Orlando, Florida, spirits of 'pleasure' and 'leisure' can be clearly attached to the vacation industry that is so predominant there.

Dawson differentiates between 'points of entry' and 'dominant features' of a region. A point of entry would be a historic event, such as the slave trade, that gave sin a place in the community, thus enabling demonic forces to establish a foothold. According to Dawson, geographical areas have dominant features that can either be used to glorify God or to advance Satan and sinful activity and obstruct the gospel from being spread.

He uses his own city of Los Angeles as an example, saying that communication is the dominant feature there. As proof, he offers evidence that Southern California is one of the world's largest centers of pornography distribution and the home of the film and television industry, which has sent messages propagating sinful lifestyles around the world. On the other hand, Los Angeles is also home to some major Christian ministries, such as World Vision, the Trinity Broadcasting Network and the International Church of the Foursquare Gospel.

Miami, Florida. Larry Lea calls together the Christians of the city for a 'Prayer Breakthrough.' He insists that there be unity among the pastors – which has never been easy to achieve in Miami. He says that without unity there cannot be effective warfare. Pastors from 430 local churches respond and join him. The Miami Herald calls it the largest pastoral gathering in the area's history.

More than 10,000 people join Lea for prayer at the Miami Arena. There is repentance and praise and worship. Lea identifies four levels of territorial warfare:

1. Principalities. These are individual demon spirits.
2. Powers. This group includes the captains of teams of spirits (such as Legion in Mark 5:9).
3. Rulers of darkness. This group includes regional spirits.
4. Strongmen. These dominate wickedness in high places and oversee the other levels of demonic activity.

On the first two nights, Lea and the 10,000 Christians rebuke the regional spirits. Lea and the Miami area pastors identify spirits of fear, religiosity, violence, drugs, witchcraft, discouragement and greed. 'We declare that these spirits will not dominate this area,' says Lea from the podium. 'We declare that the spirit of fear will not rule in this city.'

On the final night, Lea leads a spiritual attack against the strongman of 'greed,' which he discerns as ruling the area.

'Discernment and unity – you must have both if you are going to be able to do this,' says Lea about spiritual warfare on a territorial level.

Lea conducts 'Prayer Breakthroughs' around the country. He says this type of intercession and spiritual action will become more visible and more intense in the 1990s. And it will lead to evangelism, according to Lea. 'Once the spirits that dominate an area are held back,' he says, 'the gospel will be able to get in. People will turn to Jesus.'

The New Testament makes it clear that Jesus and His disciples dealt with demons. On one occasion, Jesus cast a legion of demons into a herd of swine (Mark 5:1-15). He also charged His disciples to cast out demons (Matt. 10:7-8), and the book of Acts records their confrontations with evil spirits. Their ministry is used as an example to indicate that we should be doing the same today.

But when it comes to dealing with territorial principalities, it is not quite so clear what we should be doing. C. Peter Wagner says one of the many questions regarding territorial spirits is whether or not Christians can confront them directly.

'It can be very dangerous,' says Wagner. 'There are horror stories where people's ministries were wiped out when they tried this.'

In West Africa, Wagner says, a pastor flippantly ordered a tree cut down that had long been called 'the devil's tree' and identified with a local witch doctor. The second the tree was felled, the pastor dropped dead. Was it demons? Wagner sees a possible connection but warns that 'there is still much research to be done in this area.'

Bringing down territorial spirits identified with specific geographical areas is a fairly new concept. Vineyard Christian Fellowship pastor John Wimber questions the lack of direct biblical references and the lack of instruction in the Bible as to how to handle principalities.

Wagner suggests that once church history is thoroughly studied on the matter, evidence likely will be found that this sort of spiritual warfare has existed all along, particularly in the area of intercessory prayer.

Dawson says that the key to breaking spiritual strongholds is not to focus on Satan – though we can uncover the devil's works – but to focus on Jesus Christ and the power of the Holy Spirit. Dawson says the choice is either revival or judgment.

Los Angeles, California. John Dawson meditates on Leviticus 26:31: 'I will lay your cities waste and bring your sanctuaries to desolation.' Was God talking about his city? About Los Angeles?

Prompted by the Holy Spirit, Dawson begins to intercede for his city and gets others to do the same. He prays with his mother, Joy Dawson, and a pastor friend, Dan Sneed. Mostly unfamiliar Bible passages come to their minds. They look them up. Each one pronounces severe judgment. The three cry out to God for mercy, entering into a 'season of travail' of ongoing intercessory prayer.

More than six months pass. Dawson is busily involved

in planning a massive outreach bringing together more than 6,000 Christian missionaries to witness about Jesus to people attending the 1984 Summer Olympics in Los Angeles.

On the last day of the Olympic outreach, Dawson receives a phone call from Jack Hayford. 'John, I am calling our church to pray with special urgency today,' he says, explaining that he and others are sensing that a major catastrophe could be averted only through fervent prayer.

There are no visible signs of disaster in Los Angeles that day, no natural calamity. The news media reports of possible terrorist attacks have not yet materialized. But Dawson knows in his heart that Christians need to pray as never before. He begins a huge telephone prayer network.

The 6,000 missionaries gather at a park for a massive prayer meeting. Christians from more than 30 nations intercede for the city. With eyes shut and hands lifted, they pray for God's mercy and protection.

Simultaneously, Christians around the city pray. There is no disaster, no terrorist attack. Instead, thousands of people listen to the Word being preached and open themselves to the moving of the Holy Spirit.

'I believe that in that summer of 1984 something terrible was about to happen in Los Angeles,' says Dawson. 'It was averted through the repentance, obedience and earnest prayer of thousands of Christians.'

Spiritual warfare is activated on the international level, the national level, the community level and in the church, according to Dawson. But it also involves every neighborhood and every household. 'Warfare begins on a personal level,' he says, 'and escalates through layers of increasing difficulty.'

This is not a 'demon under every rock' theology. Neither is it a formula or ritual that works at the snap of a finger. Rather, it is an acknowledgment of the unseen battle and a willingness to persist in the warfare until victory is seen. Dawson stresses the importance of 'travailing' through prayer until there is a breakthrough. Sometimes this can take days, months, even years.

This decade promises to be a time of active spiritual warfare, with Christians being more involved than ever and with Christians having a better understanding of the ramifications of cosmic-level confrontations.

But for Dawson, Lea, Wagner, Bernal and others, the focus is not on the battle itself but on the result: salvation of the lost, deliverance of people bound by sin, a deeper relationship with the Holy Spirit for Christians.

The strategies for spiritual warfare appear to be calling some to the front lines. Wagner proposes that not everyone will be involved with direct confrontations with high-level spirits on a regular basis. Others have varying approaches and degrees of caution. But everyone agrees that intercessory prayer for a household, a neighborhood, a city, a nation, a region is the vital cog, the initial seed that makes a breakthrough possible. And the many voices of prayer around the world are indeed producing dramatic changes both on a cosmic and a natural level.

3

Territorial Spirits

by C. Peter Wagner

One of the first pieces I published on territorial spirits appeared as a short section in my book How to Have a Healing Ministry without Making Your Church Sick *(Regal Books). Without developing theological fine points, I basically wanted to gather together some of the field experiences of individuals ministering in different parts of the world as case studies of what we might be looking at as we move to engage in strategic-level spiritual warfare.*

In many places a key to the spread of the gospel is the power encounter. But there is a subcategory of power encounter that has great potential for accelerating world evangelization and about which Christian leaders seem to know relatively little. I refer to breaking the power of territorial spirits.

We read in 2 Corinthians 4:4 that Satan has successfully blinded the minds of unbelievers so that they cannot receive the gospel. This undoubtedly refers to individuals, but could it also refer to territories? Could it mean nations? States? Cities? Cultural groups? Tribes? Social networks? In the parable of the sower, Jesus said that the seed of the Word falling on the road produces no fruit, because 'Satan comes immediately and takes away the word that was sown in their hearts' (Mark 4:15). Church growth theory has long ago recognized the phenomenon of resistant peoples. Could it be that at least some of that resistance may be caused by the direct working of demonic forces?

Sumrall's Greatest Battle

To illustrate let's look at a dramatic event that occurred a number of years ago in the Philippines under the ministry of Lester Sumrall. He reports that he went on an extended evangelistic mission to the Philippines, because he felt he heard a direct word from God telling him to go and that great things would happen. But after five months of preaching, only five people were saved. Obviously, something was wrong.

One night Sumrall heard a radio report mention an inmate in the Bilibid Prison named Clarita Villanueva. Some unseen creature apparently was biting her, leaving deep teeth marks on her neck, arms and legs. She frequently behaved like an animal, biting, scratching and kicking the doctors. The media featured her case. During the radio broadcast Sumrall felt God calling him to go to the prison and cast demons out of her. He prayed all that night, and the next day asked permission from the mayor. The mayor said that she was a witch and that no one was allowed near her. But after Sumrall had signed a legal release, he was permitted to go to her cell.

The moment he saw her, one of the demons spoke in English (although the woman herself could not speak English); 'I don't like you!' It cursed Sumrall, God and the blood of Christ. Sumrall says, 'I went into the greatest battle of my life,' but through the power of the Holy Spirit he got rid of the demons and led her to Christ. Sumrall reports that '150,000 people experienced salvation because of this great miracle' and 'From that day the Philippines has had revival.'[1]

I am not sure that we know for a fact whether the power of

one or more territorial spirits was broken at that time. But in recent years the rate of church growth has greatly accelerated in the Philippines. I cite this event because I believe it is a type of ministry that we should take more seriously than many of us have in the past. I should think that, using Clarita Villanueva's deliverance as a hypothesis that some cosmic changes may have taken place, would be a potentially fruitful avenue of research for evangelism and church growth.

Argentine Spirits

Among my personal circle of friends, the one who has had the most experience in dealing with territorial spirits is Argentine Omar Cabrera, pastor of the Vision of the Future Church. A unique feature of his church is that it is decentralized, meeting in 40 or more cities simultaneously throughout the central region of Argentina. Omar and his wife, Marfa, travel 7,000 miles a month, mostly by automobile, leading the church, which numbers some 90,000. How does he move into a new location for his church?

His general practice, after the potential site is selected, is to check into a hotel and seclude himself alone in a room in prayer and fasting. It usually takes the first two or three days to allow the Holy Spirit to cleanse him, to help him disassociate himself, and to identify with Jesus. He feels he 'leaves the world' and is in another realm where the spiritual warfare takes place. The attacks of the enemy at times become fierce. He has even seen some spirits in physical form. His objective is to learn their names and break their power over the city. It usually takes five to eight days, but sometimes more. Once he spent 45 days in conflict. But when he finishes, people in his meetings frequently are saved and healed even before he preaches or prays for them.

I have previously described the tremendous growth of churches in Argentina today and the power evangelism that is accompanying it. I have talked for hours with friends like Omar Cabrera and Edgardo Silvoso listening to them analyze what seems to be behind the extraordinary moving of God in that nation since the Falkland Islands war of 1982. One hypothesis relates directly to the type of cosmic struggles I am describing here.

Back in the days when Juan Peron ruled the country, he used as his chief advisor a male witch, Jose Lopez Rega, who was a high priest of the Macumba strain of spiritism. Silvoso reports that Lopez Rega was the *de facto* power of the government, infiltrating the media, the business world and the military. A wave of demonic activity swept the country. People were giving testimonies on national television as to how they were helped by Macumba. Unfortunately, the evangelical community was ill-equipped to deal with all of this. As Silvoso told me, 'We had sound doctrine, but we were powerless to combat demonic forces.' Churches had not grown significantly in decades.

It is rumored that when Lopez Rega left the government, he placed a curse on Argentina that resulted in the inhuman atrocities under the role of the military from 1976 to 1981. Civil rights were unknown. Thousands of people simply disappeared, now known to be raped, tortured, brutally murdered and thrown into secret mass graves, or dumped into the river. Then the change came in 1982. What exactly happened in the cosmic realm in 1982 we do not yet know. But, more than in any other place I know, the most prominent Christian leaders in Argentina, such as Omar Cabrera, Carlos Annacondia, Hector Gimenez and others, overtly challenge and curse Satan and his demonic forces both in private prayer and on public platforms. The nation as a whole apparently is engaged in a world-class power encounter.

Spirits in Other Lands

When I first met Omar Cabrera several years ago, I wondered if his ministry of breaking the power of territorial spirits was unique or whether others might know something about it as well. Since then my research has uncovered several reports from different parts of the world that seem to confirm the reality of what we are talking about. For example, Timothy Warner of Trinity Evangelical Divinity School believes that pioneer missionaries especially need to be prepared to break the power of spirits that rule territories. He relates incidents from missionaries to Indians in Canada and Papua New Guinea where this was actually done.[2]

Paul Yonggi Cho describes an interview with an American Presbyterian chaplain who had experienced a dry, fruitless ministry among the military in Germany, but in Korea 'suddenly heaven opens and the Spirit pours out.' Cho says that in Germany 'the powers of the sky were not broken because the German church did not pray.' In Korea the 'atmosphere of the air' is different, because the cosmic evil powers have been broken. In Korea, Cho says, 'There is not so much pollution as we are a praying church.' He cites the early morning prayer meetings, the all-night prayer meetings and the prayer mountains that are all very much a part of Korean church life.[3]

Jack M. Chisholm, pastor of the Glendale, California, Presbyterian Church, made an investigative trip to Korea. Among many lessons for growth and renewal he learned was his newfound conviction that we need to be able to 'tackle the strongholds, to break down the towers, and to set people free.' He believes that the new wave of the power of the Holy Spirit that many of us are seeing 'will break the backs of demonic institutions that hold nations as well as people in bondage.[4]

Bill Jackson tells in *World Christian* magazine of a missionary couple in Thailand, who saw no fruit for years until they decided to set one day a week aside to go into the woods and engage the territorial spirits in warfare. A wave of conversions followed. Jackson believes that thousands of unreached peoples are currently under the direct thumb of Satan, and 'The gospel won't go forward among these peoples until we bind the spirits that bind them, whether those deceptive forces be Islam, Hinduism, or any of a myriad of others.[5]

In recent years churches have been growing rapidly in Brazil, but very slowly in neighboring Uruguay. A missionary who met Ralph Mahoney of World MAP had a strange experience while distributing tracts in a small town on the border of Brazil and Uruguay, where the main street divided the two nations. He found that on the Uruguay side no one would accept the tracts, while they received them gratefully on the Brazilian side of the street. And individuals who refused them on the Uruguay side would change their attitude and taken them on the Brazilian side. The missionary's interpretation was that 'in crossing the street they were passing out from under the covering of darkness in Uruguay into a country that had experienced, in part, the removing of the covering.'[6]

What Are Their Names?

Mark I. Bubeck sees Satan as the commander-in-chief of the forces of darkness, leading a hierarchical structure of evil spirits. The most powerful are *principalities* or *princes*. Bubeck understands them to have vast power and a certain degree of independence of action. Under them are *powers* 'probably more numerous and somewhat less independent and powerful than the princes.' Next are the *rulers of darkness* who serve as lower grade officers. Finally come the *wicked spirits* or *demons*.[7]

Paul Lehmann, a missionary to Zaire with Christian and Missionary Alliance, recently published a list of the names of demons he cast out of a witch doctor, Tata Pembele. They included Guard of the Ancestors, Spirit of Travel, Feeder of the Dead, Rescuer from Sorcery, Voice of the Dead, Spreader of Illness, Paralyzer, Destroyer in Water, Healer and many others. Through them the witch doctor had exercised great power.[8]

Witches in the Los Angeles area chant to Isis, Astarte, Hecate, Demeter, Kali and Innana. Others bow to Cerridwen, Mother of Earth and Cernunnos, Father of the Woodlands. Paul Kauffman has identified a chief spirit of Thailand as Narai. Indians in the Andes acknowledge the power of Pachamama, Inti and Viracocha. Some Mexicans feel that the Aztec war god Huitzilopochtil still exercies power.

The names of two territorial spirits are apparently mentioned in Daniel 10. He speaks of an angel of God who was coming to minister to him, but who was delayed because of spiritual warfare with 'the prince of the kingdom of Persia' (v. 13; see also v. 20) and who later expected a similar battle with the 'prince of Greece' (v. 20). Paul refers to them as principalities and powers and 'spiritual hosts of wickedness in the heavenly places' (Eph. 6:12).

The Spirit of Merigildo

Edgardo Silvoso was the speaker at one of our recent prayer retreats held at Lake Avenue Congregational Church in Pasadena, California. One of his topics was spiritual warfare. He told how in 1985 he and some friends had taken a map, drawn a circle with a 100-mile radius around his Harvest Evangelism leadership training center near Rosario, Argentina, and discovered that there were 109 towns within the circle with no evangelical church. They then found that in a town called Arroyo Seco a warlock named Merigildo had long exercised great power. He had trained 12 disciples, and when he died, he transferred his power to a spring of water. Once this was discovered, Christian leaders of the area, Pentecostal and non-Pentecostal, gathered together for a prayer meeting to do spiritual warfare. Silvoso reports that it was the most powerful prayer meeting he had ever attended. They took dominion over the area in the name of Jesus.

Six of them then went to the headquarters of Merigildo in Arroyo Seco, Silvoso among them. They served public notice that he was defeated by the blood of Christ, pointed their car toward the headquarters building, and broke the evil power in the name of Jesus.

The results? In less than three years after Merigildo's power was broken, 82 of the 109 towns had an evangelical church, and more were rapidly being planted.

There is so much more to learn about resisting the devil. We have many questions and not enough answers. But one answer that we do have is that Jesus is building His Church, and the power of the Holy Spirit is more than sufficient so that 'the gates of Hades shall not prevail against it' (Matt. 16:18).

Endnotes

1. Lester Sumrall, 'Deliverance: Setting the Captives Free,' *World Harvest*, July/Aug. 1986, p. 7.
2. Timothy M. Warner, 'Power Encounter with the Demonic,' *Evangelism on the Cutting Edge*, Robert E. Coleman, ed. (Old Tappan, NJ: Fleming H. Revell Co., 1986), pp. 98, 99.
3. Paul Yonggi Cho and C. Peter Wagner, eds., *Church Growth Manual No. 1*, Seoul: Church Growth International, 1986, p. 41.
4. Jack M. Chisholm, 'Go to Korea and Learn From Them,' *The Forerunner*, June 1984, p. 23.
5. Bill Jackson, 'Waging War,' *World Christian*, Jan./Feb. 1985, p. 11.
6. Ralph Mahoney, 'The Covering of Darkness,' *World MAP Digest*, Mar./Apr. 1983, p. 3.
7. Mark I. Bubeck, *The Adversary* (Chicago: Moody Press, 1975), pp. 72, 73.
8. Paul Lehmann, 'Invading Satan's Territory,' *The Alliance Witness*, Mar. 18, 1987, p. 19.

4

Dealing with Territorial Demons

by Timothy M. Warner

Timothy Warner introduced a course on power encounter at Trinity Evangelical Divinity School, Deerfield, Illinois, where he is a missions professor, and the response was dramatic. He discovered that many traditional, rather conservative evangelicals had a deep desire to learn about the reality of the spirit world, a subject somewhat taboo in academic circles. Warner, a former missionary to Sierra Leone, not only developed the theoretical side in the classroom, but also engaged in a rather extensive deliverance ministry himself.

In recent years a number of other evangelical professors have introduced similar subjects into their curriculum, stimulated to a significant degree by Warner's pioneering efforts. Many of these professors contributed to a volume which I edited along with Douglas Pennoyer, Wrestling With Dark Angels *(Regal Books, 1990), and which I strongly recommend to those who desire more information. This brief chapter contains material which Timothy Warner presented to Fuller Theological Seminary in the 1989 annual Church Growth Lectures. His over all topic was 'Power Encounter in World Evangelization.'*

Excerpted from 'The Power Encounter and World Evangelization,' The 1988 Church Growth Lectureship at Fuller Seminary School of World Mission © 1988 by permission of the author.

An area of power encounter which is just beginning to be taken seriously is the confrontation of demons associated with specific locations or geo-political units. The whole concept of the gods of the nations in the Old Testament and the references in Daniel to the Prince of Persia and the Prince of Greece (Dan. 10:13, 20) provide us with a biblical insight into this, and Jesus' statement about binding the strong man (Matt. 12:29) may also apply.

I have come to believe that Satan does indeed assign a demon or a corps of demons to every geo-political unit in the world and that they are among the principalities and powers against whom we wrestle.

This concept first came up in the missionary context when I read of a new missionary going into an American Indian village in Canada. A veteran of such ministry told him that he had better be prepared to do battle with the demon of the village on his arrival. The young missionary's world view and training had not prepared him for such concepts, and they just moved in. It was not long, however, before his wife became ill and had to be flown out. The young man was standing alone in his cabin with his back to the stove to keep warm when he heard an awful noise that seemed to be coming from the stove pipe. Suddenly something jumped on his back; and, although he could not see anything, he was barely able to stagger to a chair to sit down. The 'thing' identified itself as the demon of the village, and the battle was joined.

The missionary knew enough to claim his position in Christ, and he said 'All right Satan, you guardian angel of Borchet, let's have it out. Jesus Christ sent me here. I might die, but I am not leaving, and with the Lord are the issues of death.' After thirty minutes of struggle, claiming the legal victory of Calvary and all the while gasping for breath, the demon left as it had come, and the missionary stayed on to carry out his ministry.

How this may relate to many other missionary problems, we simply do not know because it has not even been seen as in the realm of possibility. More recently, however, some other things have called this to our attention. For example, there is a town on the border between Brazil and Uruguay in which the main street is the international border. One side of the street is in Brazil and the other side in Uruguay. Ralph Mahoney of World MAP tells of a missionary who was in this town passing out tracts. On the Uruguay side of the street people were very unresponsive; but when he crossed over to the Brazil side, a person who had refused a tract on the Uruguay side of the street now received the tract and even thanked him profusely for it. His curiosity aroused, he tested several more people and found the same pattern.

Peter Wagner reports that:

> later as [the missionary] was praying about the incident, the words of Jesus came to his mind: 'No one can enter a strong man's house and plunder his goods, unless he first binds the strong man, and then he will plunder the house' (Mark 3:27). Could it be that the 'strong man' on the Brazilian side had been bound while the 'strong man' on the Uruguayan side was still exercising power? (Wagner 1986, 84).

This concept is what seems to be a key factor in the amazing revival movement that is taking place in Argentina. Ed Silvoso, writing in *Global Church Growth*, reports that 3000, and maybe as many as 8000, persons per day are making decisions for Christ in Argentina. The one element in the evangelistic approach which seems to be new is the role of prayer. Not only are there prayer brigades organized to support the evangelists and prayer as a prominent part of the services, at least one of the evangelists will spend from several days up to two weeks in fasting and prayer to bind the 'strong man' or the 'prince' who controls the darkness of that particular 'cosmos' (Silvoso 1987, 5). As soon as the Lord gives him the assurance that this has been done, he begins preaching; and the results speak for themselves. This is a dramatic illustration of S.D. Gordon's statement, 'Intercession is winning the victory over the chief, and service is taking the field after the chief is driven off' (Gordon 1904, 17).

There are other elements to the evangelistic ministries in Argentina which help to account for the response. One of them is the use of an intensive care tent where the demonized are ministered to. It appears that most evangelicals have chosen to simply avoid confrontation with or ministry to spiritists, but where that challenge is being met head on, God's power is clearly demonstrated and many are drawn to Him.

I am not suggesting that we can go around binding the spirits that control any area we choose. I do think, however, that when God commissions a missionary to minister in a particular location, the missionary and the church can claim the authority of our Lord over every spirit of the enemy claiming that territory for Satan.

5

Dealing with the Enemy in Society

by R. Arthur Mathews

Arthur Mathews, an internationally-known missionary leader with Overseas Missionary Fellowship (formerly China Inland Mission), has been on the front lines of spiritual warfare long enough to speak with authority. He was born in China of missionary parents, raised in Australia, served in the Indian Army in World War II, was a missionary in China's interior and suffered four years of house arrest with his wife and baby in Communist China. In this chapter Mathews gives his views on how spirit powers of evil might be affecting segments of society.

Our generation has eyed with increasing trepidation the successive waves of evil which have infiltrated world society. The foundations of morality are being undermined. The central influences of life are being taken over by men from the bottom levels of society in contrast to earlier generations. God's authority in society is mediated from the top in the punishing of evil and the rewarding of good. But when control is taken over by the men at the bottom, we may be sure that the devil is in it. Thus permissiveness and situation ethics have blurred the

Excerpted from *Born for Battle* by R. Arthur Mathews © 1978 OMF Books with permission of the publisher.

issues, weakened the power to discern evil under its camouflage of misrepresentation, and then sapped the will to resist. Religious heretical sects are multiplying and gaining power. Drugs that blow the mind have taken captive many of the upcoming generation. Enemy attack has brought its casualties in every part of corporate life – the family, the educational system, the judicial system, and even the church. The pattern is to compromise or to break away from God's fixed moral standards.

What all this is saying is that, the 'principalities and powers in heavenly places' have mustered their unseen array, rigged their Trojan horse, infiltrated society, and opened the gates for a flood of evil to take over.

The Bible has alerted us to the possibility of supernatural evil powers establishing themselves in local cultures and then controlling life and custom. The messenger of the church at Pergamos is reminded of the grim fact that he dwells 'where Satan's seat is.' The obvious implication of this is that Satan's infiltration had reached its intended climax in the establishment of a control center on earth, from which to direct the powers of darkness in their opposition to God's purposes of grace.

Questions again flood our minds. How do these spirit powers exert their influence in society? Where do they get in? Is there a distinctive *modus operandi* that would help us identify them? What can or what should we be doing to control and prevent their intrusion? Since God is sovereign and omnipotent, is it not our place to let Him deal with these supernatural powers in His own time and way?

The Bible must have answers to these questions, and it does. But the terrifying fact of a hostile world of evil and malicious spirits paralyzes many Christians into inactivity and unwillingness to seek our Biblical answers and to apply them. Edith Schaeffer says that 'there is a deafness, a blindness, an insensitivity among many Christians, for they refuse to recognize the war in which they are involved. They are letting the enemy attack and score victories without resistance.'

There are many clear indications of Satan's motives and methods given us in the Bible, if only we would heed them. He is the arch-deceiver, adversary, accuser, the father of lies, and a 'murderer from the beginning.' His central purpose is to pull God from His throne in the minds of men and to take that throne himself. To do this, he scored a flying start over the whole human race through our forefather Adam. Having won Adam over to his side, his fight is to maintain his advantage over mankind. To do this, he has his control centers run by men who have rejected God's control, the world's strong natural leaders who want to shape history after their own ideals; and in smaller communities the witch doctors, and leaders in heretical sects. We have a good example of this in the worship of the goddess Artemis (Diana, KJV). In modern history, ancestor worship in China and Japan are other examples. On the other side, the Christian must make the reconquest of the ground yielded to the devil his invariable study and be committed to the goals of his Captain.

However, what we are seeing today is the sacrificing of the localized culture controls. The once powerful Lama system of Tibet has been completely broken up in order to bring the Tibetans into the larger orbit of atheistic communism. Thus some of the centuries-old cultures are being forced to yield to the mold of one great anti-God system, so the devil's strong natural leader will have a unified world under his control. Satan is realizing that time is beyond his control and is running out on him. This multiplies his fury, especially as he realizes how limited is his success in welding the nations together. He seems to have more success in fragmenting Christians than he does in uniting his own side.

It seems to me that the shuffling of loyalties among the nations of the world's unholy alliances is evidence of God's working to scatter and confuse rebellious elements as He did at the Tower of Babel. This in itself is a guide for us as we pray for 'kings and all in authority.' We would see these things if we were watching unto prayer. We miss them because we confine our living and interest to earth and ignore our responsibilities in the heavenlies. We have the man's-eye view, instead of communing long and deeply with the Lord to get the

Lord's-eye view. Should we not encourage each other to gain imperial perspective in our praying?

We look out on wars and rumors of war, political and economic instability, visa limitations on missionaries in some countries, and every kind of obstacle put in the way of the Church to prevent her from fulfilling her commission. And how do we react to these things? Yes, we do go to prayer, but generally our praying centers around the missionary and ignores the powers that arrange these things. Consequently our praying, like King Canute's command to the waves to come no further up the beach, does nothing. Barriers are not moved by God's omnipotence until the believer takes the initiative and stands his ground in the heavenly places to engage the powers of evil that are directly the cause of the ground-level troubles, and resists them in the name of the Victor of Calvary.

What does Paul do in the scary situation at Ephesus? He gets together with Gaius and Aristarchus, or whoever was available, and together they take their position in Christ in the heavenlies and wrestle with and withstand the powers of evil that are manipulating the willing puppets on the streets. Immediately there is a break in the situation. Empowered in the Lord and in the strength of His might and panoplied in heavenly armor, they force Satan to yield ground, and the town clerk quietens the screaming mob.

Such resistance against supernatural powers is not done boastfully or presumptuously, but humbly as befits those who realize that they have no might in themselves and that they owe everything to the grace and power of God. The exercise is not a call for self-advertisement as some would make it. It is the ordained function of those who are in Christ and, I think we should add, of those who are filled with the Spirit. God does not commission men not filled with the Spirit to fight His battles. Paul was filled with the Holy Spirit when he confronted Elymas the sorcerer and exposed the devil's attack and defeated him (Acts 13:9). It is not to be passed over that the command to be filled with the Spirit comes in the context of the Christian's walk on earth and his warfare in the heavenlies.

6

Understanding Principalities and Powers

by Thomas B. White

Thomas White is a Conservative Baptist pastor and the founding president of Frontline Ministries of Corvallis, Oregon. For years he has specialized in strategic-level spiritual warfare dealing with both the theoretical and practical aspects. He is much in demand as a seminar leader on spiritual warfare as well as a consultant to groups attempting to deal with territorial spirits in their cities or other areas.

In this chapter White analyzes the nature of high ranking forces of evil and gives practical suggestions as to the kind of ministry which will be most effective in combatting them.

The term 'principalities and powers' evokes all kinds of mystical mental images. We think of giant, spiritual beings with capes and swords who roam about wreaking havoc on innocent people. Darth Vader of Star Wars fame would certainly come close, a mythical being with a secret source of dark power. Spiritual warfare demands that we gain a working understanding of what these powers really are. My intent here is to make simple an obscure subject. What exactly do we 'struggle' against? Who, or what, are these 'principalities and powers'?

Excerpted from *The Believer's Guide to Spiritual Warfare* by Thomas B. White, Ann Arbor, Michigan, Servant Publications © 1990, by permission of the author.

We know from Ephesians 1:21 and 6:12, and Colossians 1:6 and 2:15, that these are fallen spiritual beings that operate in Satan's domain, opposing the redemptive purposes of God. Often the question arises: where did these evil beings come from? Three separate theories are usually mentioned: they are the disembodied spirits of a pre-Adamic race, destroyed by God (this idea fits with the 'gap theory' of creation); they are the 'Nephilim' of Genesis 6, the disembodied spirits of a mutant race created by the mating of angels and humans; last, they are of the original angelic creation that fell with Lucifer. I believe the last theory is correct, that we are dealing with fallen angels.

The study of both Old and New Testaments, with additional evidence from Apocryphal texts, reveals three categories of fallen angels: 1) those angels who fell originally with Lucifer at the time of his rebellion and who are still active in the deception and affliction of people; 2) the 'sons of God' (angelic beings) of Genesis 6:2 who committed such abominable acts of immorality with the 'daughters of men' (women), they were 'bound with everlasting chains for judgment on the great Day' (Jude 6); 3) angelic beings who were given charge to watch and rule over certain groupings of mankind. This latter grouping is the least familiar to us. Moses spoke of them:

> When the Most High gave the nations their inheritance, when he divided all mankind, he set up boundaries for the peoples *according to the number of the sons of Israel.* (Dt. 32:8, emphasis mine.)

According to the Septuagint text and recent scholarship, the clearer rendering here is 'sons of God,' angelic beings (cf. Job 38:7). Daniel 4:13 and 17 call these powers the 'Watchers.' Who are they? I believe they were angels of a high order endowed with divine authority and appointed to watch over certain segments of humanity. In short, they were spiritual governors. Scripture speaks of the 'council of Yahweh,' heavenly beings who carry out the divine will (1 Kings 22:19; Ps

89:6, 7). In light of the Genesis 6 and Jude passages, it seems that it was possible for these powers to lose their positions of authority (Jude 6), and to come under satanic influence (cf. Ps 82:1, 2). Thus, there are powers who seem to have fallen after the fact of Lucifer's rebellion, tempted by their own pride, and usurping positions not ordained by God. D.S. Russell, a scholar of Jewish apocalyptic, captures what may have happened in the spiritual realm:

> There gradually grew up, no doubt under the influence of foreign thought, the notion that the angels to whom God had given authority over the nations and over the physical universe itself, had outstripped their rightful authority and had taken the power into their own hands ... They refused any longer to take their orders from God, but were either rulers in their own right or were prepared to take their orders from someone other than God who, like themselves, had rebelled against the Almighty.[1]

Dualism, however, was foreign to Old Testament theology. The existence of a separate realm of supernatural evil was not clearly perceived. Gradually a post-exilic understanding developed that these powers were separate from God, a source of evil unto themselves. The book of Daniel best reveals this understanding. In my view, these powers coincide with the pagan gods and goddesses worshiped by the Greeks and Romans, territorial deities or 'princes' (Dan. 10:13, 20) who sought the worship of men. Others became connected with the worship of certain planets and astral bodies (Zeus, Mars, Hermes). Thus, these forces became part of the domain of darkness, manipulated by Satan, the mastermind of deceit.

Hell's Corporate Headquarters

Paul brings light to the topic by depicting the powers as organized in a hierarchy of rulers/principalities (*archai*), authorities (*exousia*), powers (*dunamis*), and spiritual forces of evil (*kosmokratoras*). It is reasonable to assume the authority structure here is arranged in descending order. Daniel 10:13 and 20 unveil the identity of the *archai* as high level satanic princes set over nations and regions of the earth. The word *exousia* carries a connotation of both supernatural and natural government. In the Apostle's understanding, there were supernatural forces that 'stood behind' human structures. Paul no doubt is voicing the Jewish apocalyptic notion of cosmic beings who were given authority by God to arbitrate human affairs. Presumably, the *dunamis* operate within countries and cultures to influence certain aspects of life. The *kosmokratoras* are the many types of evil spirits that commonly afflict people, e.g., spirits of deception, divination, lust, rebellion, fear, and infirmity. These, generally, are the evil powers confronted and cast out in most deliverance sessions. Even among them there is ranking, the weaker spirits subservient to stronger ones.

Until the Judgment, God allows these forces to remain active. The world functions in the tension of a transitional time when victory over darkness has been won, but the redeemed continue to struggle against evil. God allows the adversary to act as tempter and tester. For the individual Christian who submits to God, the schemes of evil serve as tougheners of faith.

These insidious powers continue to work through human governments, religions, and powerful personalities to keep people in bondage to legalism, social ideology, and moral compromise. Their role is to pollute the minds and pervert the wills of people, diverting them from redemption, holding them hostage to the father of lies. When we describe evil at this level, we are in a sense describing the Board Room of Hell, acknowledging that there are high ranking C.E.O.s (Chief Executive Officers) responsible for major movements of deception and destruction in our world. For example, there may be principalities that promote such things as the proliferation of New Age metaphysics, the rise of ritualistic satanism, the production and provision of drugs, the practice of terrorism, sexual perversion, and pornography. There are probably strong, ancient principalities that work through the Hindu caste system of

India. Millions are held in bondage to this system of religious legalism.

In 1988, I did some teaching for a missions organization in Colombia. I will never forget the day I arrived at the jungle compound that housed some four hundred Christian workers. By the first evening, I began to notice a crushing weight of oppression closing in around me. I felt unusually vulnerable and threatened. No, it was not just the intense heat and humidity of the jungle climate, nor was it the usual cultural adjustment. As I worked that week, I learned that the compound was surrounded by four major, militant influences: 1) armed Marxist guerrillas fighting to control the country; 2) routes for the transfer of raw coca out of the jungles and into the hands of the cocaine drug lords; 3) tribal Indian groups that practiced witchcraft; 4) militant groups who were vehemently opposed to missionaries.

I also found out that the year before I arrived, a local Colombian had murdered a missionary woman, and had vowed to kill again as soon as he could get out of prison. By the third or fourth day in this atmosphere, I felt I was being engulfed by an oppressive confusion that made it difficult to function. During the night, I battled as never before with false accusation and discouragement. Was it just my imagination? Was it the stress of a difficult assignment, added to the rigors of life in the jungle? Partially, perhaps. But I have concluded that I and the others at the compound were the targets of spiritual forces opposed to our purpose. Because my task was to instruct the other workers in discernment and spiritual authority, I was a particular target for spiritual attack, the effect of which lingered for weeks after my return home.

Far too many missionary candidates have been sent into such situations untrained in the skills of spiritual warfare, only to return from the field battered and defeated. It is time to take seriously the biblical worldview that depicts front line ministry in terms of armed warfare.

In the spring of 1989 I was privileged to take my family to Israel for ministry and touring. Sitting with the leadership team of a Jewish-Christian congregation in Tel Aviv, I posed the question, 'What is it really like being a Jewish believer in this place?' I was ill-prepared for the length and intensity of the response. All of the social, political, and economic discrimination you can imagine was a part of daily life for them. But beyond this, I began to discern the deeper spiritual dynamics that make Christian life in Israel so difficult.

Over the next week, I began to isolate the principalities and powers at work: 1) a militant, spiritual rejection of Jewish Christians by Orthodox groups that is rooted in the rejection of Yeshua as Messiah; 2) a curse of destruction spoken by Muslims committed to the Intifada, the uprising against Israel; 3) a powerful influence of secularism among the non-religious Jews, especially in Tel Aviv; 4) the influx of New Age thought and occultism that seek to fill the need of the Jews for spiritual meaning. The longer we lingered in this land, the more real and intense these influences became to us. Anyone with any sensitivity who walks the streets and corridors of Jerusalem can sense the presence of the Lord and the eternal significance of this city. But one also senses in the atmosphere the conflict of the various spiritual forces that operate behind the religious systems of Judaism, Christianity, and Islam, *and* behind the nationalities and cultures that thrive and strive in Jerusalem.

In any given city, region, country, or group, intelligent spiritual beings work to influence and control the attitudes and behavior of the people. That's the bad news. The good news is that the Holy Spirit is also present in every place, orchestrating the work of the faithful angels intent on revealing truth to men and women whose hearts hunger to know the living God.

Making Sense of It All

Let me summarize what I believe is an effective approach to spiritual warfare. I think spiritual warfare is a multilevel, multi-faceted phenomenon that first includes conflict between God and Satan, the angels and the demons. So little light is given us on this realm that delving into it is fascinating, but speculative.

It makes for stimulating fiction, but it is hard to get a theological handle on it.

The reality of the devil, who holds people hostage to his lies, is more clearly depicted in Scripture. In the parable of the seed and sower (Mt. 13:1-23), Jesus interprets the 'birds of the air' that steal away the seed as the demons that rob the understanding of truth from one who hears the gospel. Unmistakably, Christians have a role of prayer and authority as they co-labor with the Holy Spirit to break through the demonic blindness that separates men and women from the light of the gospel.

The New Testament describes one role of the Christian as that of soldier, both standing ground and using divine weapons to tear down strongholds of evil. Christians are to *reveal* 'to the rulers and authorities in the heavenly realms' the manifold wisdom of God to demonstrate his grace through the cross (Eph. 3:10, 11); to *expose* the designs and deeds of darkness (Eph. 5:11); to *resist* and stand actively against the devil's schemes (Eph. 6:10–18); and to *overcome* the evil one, to conquer his influence over our character (1 Jn. 2:12–14).

Most of what you and I deal with daily are the faults, foibles, and physical infirmities of our own natural selves, with all the emotional and psychological baggage that we carry through life. Beyond that, each of us has individual areas of besetting sin that nag at us and drag us down with discouraging regularity. If this were not enough, the covetousness, pleasure, and humanistic appeal of the world system presses upon us all. Now alongside, and sometimes in and through these battles, the devil takes what he can get and aggravates our unresolved emotional problems, besetting sins, and willful blunderings. We are like a finely tuned watch mechanism into which pieces of grit are dropped. What could have functioned well according to original design wears down and malfunctions due to an external, foreign influence.

Keep Your Eye on the Spy

In the same sense that a secret agent sends out a signal that merits serious attention by the opposition, so the Christian walking in obedience to the Spirit of God, abiding in prayer, and committed to the kingdom stirs enemy opposition. The stakes are higher for the veteran who can do the most damage to the domain of darkness. My premise should be clear by now: any servant of Jesus Christ who poses a serious threat to the powers of hell will be targeted and will encounter resistance, especially at times of strategic ministry. The anointed agent of Christ's kingdom must be equipped to discern and deal with the efforts of the enemy's kingdom.

A Reassuring Word

Just because we are under attack, doesn't mean we are unprotected. The loving and protective presence of God shields us moment by moment from haphazard assaults. If we sin, the indwelling Spirit immediately goes to work on our conscience to convict us of our transgression. Typically, we squirm for a while. We may rationalize why we did what we did. If this hard-hearted condition persists, we stand in danger of grieving the Spirit. But all the while, he is wooing and working on us to repent and return to him.

If we are following the Spirit and not desiring to make provision for the flesh, we will repent and be forgiven. The 'breastplate of righteousness' cleanses our conscience and covers us from the accusative arrows of the enemy. If, however, we persist in our sin, and refuse to deal with it, we may give the devil a 'foothold' (Eph. 4:27), an opening for his subtle intrusion into our lives. We need to know that God wants us forgiven and shielded from evil more than we do (see Jn. 17:15). Our Lord is greater and more powerful than all the hordes of hell. If our hearts are submitted to him in humility, if we are willing to cleanse our hands of sin and stay committed to his Lordship, then we speak the word 'devil, be gone,' and it is done (Jas 4:6–10).

Some learning is 'caught' in the course of battle, not 'taught' in a seminar or learned through a book. Today, we need to be open to allow God to train us to see the subtleties of evil. May

God be pleased to raise up men and women equipped to see as he sees, and committed to act with his authority to counteract the kingdom of darkness in our age.

Endnotes

1. Russell, D.S., *The Method of Jewish Apocalyptic*, (Philadelphia, PA: Westminster Press, 1964), pp. 237–38.

Part II

THE MINISTRY:

Pastors and Practitioners

7

Possessing Our Cities and Towns

by Jack W. Hayford

Here is a warm-hearted pastoral word from one of America's most respected pastors. Jack Hayford has seen the Church on the Way in Van Nuys, California, grow from 25 to over 7,000 under his ministry. He sees prayer as the most dynamic spiritual factor in this dramatic growth. This is the kind of biblical admonition which the Holy Spirit will use in the lives of many believers to encourage them to step out more aggressively to pray for their cities and towns and neighborhoods.

For three years now, I have had a great and distinct burden for my city of Los Angeles. Van Nuys, the community in which our congregation is located, is a part of the greater Los Angeles metropolis; and as this prayer burden has begun, I have been coming to truly *love* L.A. in a Holy Spirit-begotten way.

Through contact with other leaders, I am finding there are more and more believers across the United States and around the world who are experiencing the same compassion and intercessory burden for their cities and towns. If you are among those, then it is my prayer that you may feel even *more*

Excerpted from *Taking Hold of Tomorrow* by Jack W. Hayford, Regal Books, Ventura, California © 1989 by permission.

confirmed in the call to love and pray for your city and your church; to believe that God will bring a new tomorrow to them. As Joshua reveals in the case of Jericho and other cities, our Living Lord is 'into' city-taking. I believe He has called us all to expect we can 'possess' our cities – for *the blessing of every citizen* and for *the glory of God*.

I am not saying that I believe that any one church is the key to capturing a city with the love of God. But I do believe that *yours* might be the one that starts a trend! Dear friend, this is a perspective needed in ministering to our cities, calling us all to dimensions of love, service and witness broader than anything we've ever answered to before.

I meet many who are hearing the Spirit's call in this regard. The pursuit of such ministry is to my view, very much like the pathway outlined in principle in the book of Joshua.

Notice two texts: 1) 'And Joshua rose early in the morning...' (6:12); and 2) 'It came to pass on the seventh day that they rose early, about the dawning of the day...' (6:15).

Here's the foundational point for finding God's strategy for 'taking' our cities and towns with His love. It begins with an early start; forming bands of team-prayer – people who gird their town with intercession.

The Lord hasn't said, 'Go and barrage the city with tracts'; or even, 'Get on television – major channels and prime time! – and tell them about Me.' As valid as our literature and media witnesses may be, I think events have placed us in an hour in history where the world is less likely than ever to be impressed by slick tactics.

But there is no defense against prayer!

Heartfelt, impassioned and consistent intercessory prayer not only dissolves the power of sin's hold on human lives, it also begets among God's people a new sensitivity to the Holy Spirit. As a result, He begins to lead members to pathways of service, to answer need and pain in the city. Compassionate service in Jesus' name inevitably cultivates an openness in the worldling, a readiness to hear, to listen afresh to the message of life in Christ. Because they've been loved and served, people in the dark are more ready to consider the Light.

That's how the Holy Spirit started with us.

He awakened me one morning and said much the same thing as He said to Joshua: 'Call the people to prayer for the city; to a dimension of prayer they've not known or experienced before.' As a result, hundreds every week come to our Prayer Chapel and our midweek prayer services for extended times of prayer for our city. While people don't need to come to a specific location such as our chapel for the prayer time, such a gathering place can become the epicenter for the spiritual 'counter-quake' God wants to send. The type of prayer meetings shown, for example, in Acts chapter 4 can shake down the walls which divide people in our cities. They can demolish the invisible satanic structures that tower over the city's inhabitants.[1]

When I first sensed God's call to speak about this particular need to pray, I saw our city on the brink of destruction. How like God's words spoken to Joshua! 'I have doomed this city to destruction and all who are in it – only Rahab the harlot shall live.'[2]

I recognized this 'destruction' was not a prophecy of seismic doom. (Los Angeles is known for being threatened often by 'prophets.') I saw so clearly that we don't have to wait for an 8.0 earthquake, a 200 mile-per-hour tornado or a 100-foot flood to ravage our city. It's *already* being destroyed from within.

- *Disease* runs rampant; sickness, infection and pain are all around us.
- *Death* comes through innumerable doors; suicide, murder, abortion.
- *Despair* abounds; the growing sense of hopelessness as people's aspirations and dreams melt before them.
- *Disillusionment* deepens; children see their homes being broken as parental relationships crumble.
- *Disappointment* devastates people, businesses go under, contracts are violated.

Dishonesty. Deceit. Divorce. Dismay. *Destruction*!

People move from one city to another thinking that will solve their problems – disenchantment with life, home, wife, kids, job – and upon relocating only find that everything's different but nothing's changed.

More disappointment. More destruction. More deception. More destruction, but in another city.

Amid this, hope for tomorrow is rising.

The Lord is calling out a people who will march around their cities with their prayers. As they do, they will see the walls *broken down* which hell has built against healthy homes and happy families. The power of God can shatter the darkness that scatters families!

God is able to put the demonic powers to flight and send a holy invasion of His righteousness by the power of His Holy Spirit. He's prepared to rescue the Rahabs of our towns – the people who only wander in sin because no one has ever told them of *His* real love.

Rahab is a prophetic study. That harlot from Jericho is an example of hungry souls in the city where you live, searching for reality.

Rahab comes from a Hebrew root word meaning 'wide space, roomy.' Somehow it speaks illustratively of empty hearts, wide open to whatever of *life* might be brought to them. Though she was a prostitute when the Israeli spies came to her home, Rahab was the first to acknowledge that their God was greater than any others. Though indoctrinated in a pagan culture and trapped in her own sins, she was open to the fact that there was someone – a God *bigger* – the *Living God* – who was *better* than anything she had ever known.

Rahab's openness resulted in her life being spared, but beyond that a heartful story emerges. The Gospel of Matthew names Rahab (who, being rescued, married into the tribe of Judah) as a direct ancestor of our Lord Jesus, the Messiah![3]

How many people are there in your town who are as open as Rahab; who, if prayer broke down the walls, would respond and end up related to Jesus!

Let us join hands in prayer for our cities. They aren't hopeless – never!

This had to be written. I had to invite you to this adventure as well; in responding to your own call to possess your tomorrow, to pour out your heart in prayer for others whose tomorrows are at stake.

Something is happening among God's people.

With cities and towns,

It's happening right now.

Two kingdoms are wrestling for the city's soul.

It isn't too late to win,

if we will rise up early.

Cities deserve a tomorrow too.

They're unable to possess it for themselves.

All children of Joshua – arise!

Endnotes

1. Acts 4:23-31
2. Joshua 6:17
3. Matthew 1:5

8

Battle in the Heavenlies

by Anne Gimenez

Anne Gimenez is co-pastor of the prestigious Rock Church in Virginia Beach, Virginia, along with her husband, John. For years she has carried on an extensive ministry involving hands-on spiritual warfare. In this helpful chapter she presents convincing biblical evidence that neither the battle nor the victory in strategic-level spiritual warfare are ours. She says, 'The battle is the Lord's and the victory is already His.' She tells how she learned from God that 'my victory doesn't depend on my beating up the devil.'

The U.S. Air Force recently released pictures of the new Stealth Bombers – a sleek black aircraft stated to become a new element in our nation's defense. But actually there's nothing new about stealth bombers. I saw a couple of them years ago in Waller, Texas, near Houston.

In the wee hours of the morning, the Lord warned me of a threat to my life. But as I prayed and looked up through the darkness toward the room's closed door, I saw two angels standing like sentries on either side. Though I couldn't see their faces, they were large beings, taller than the doorway.

Excerpted from *Charisma & Christian Life* magazine, 600 Rinehart Road, Lake Mary, Florida 32746. © 1989, Strang Communications Company.

The Lord assured me that no evil would befall me; nothing was going to get through that door that night. I didn't see the angels with my spiritual eyes for long. Even so, I knew I was protected by God's own 'stealth bombers' – heavenly angels, more ready and effective and covert than any crafted machinery imaginable.

Because angels belong to the spiritual rather than the natural realm, they're not visible to the natural eye. But God's angels are as real as our nation's air force. In fact, the spiritual realm is much more real than the natural in that it is eternal and not subject to decay or death. The apostle Paul described the situation in 2 Corinthians 4:18: 'We look not at the things which are seen, but at the things which are not seen: for the things which are seen are temporal; but the things which are not seen are eternal.'

The spiritual realm is also more real in that every natural event has a spiritual origin. James 1:17 says that every good and perfect gift comes from above. All the rest – sickness, turmoil, debauchery, war, destruction – comes from rebel spirits.

As part of the spiritual realm, Satan's air force is just as real as the Lord's The prince of darkness has a host of evil spirits that rule and reign over the darkness. And there is a battle raging in the heavenlies between God's angels and Satan's angels.

Daniel 10 vividly portrays how this heavenly battle works. In this account, Daniel had been praying and fasting for three weeks, asking God for an explanation of a certain vision. After 21 days his spiritual eyes were opened and he saw an angel of the Lord who said, 'From the first day that thou didst set thine heart to understand, and to chasten thyself before thy God, thy words were heard, and I am come for thy words.' (v. 12). The angel went on to explain that 'the prince of the kingdom of Persia' had resisted him for 21 days until one of God's chief princes, Michael, came to his aid. Then the angels prevailed and broke through to give Daniel God's message.

Imagine – all this battling went on for three weeks in the heavenlies, yet Daniel didn't even know about it. Evidently heavenly battles precede earthly victories. Even so, we can identify in this account a progression of important events that began with Daniel's initiative and led up to Daniel's victory.

First of all, Daniel prayed and fasted. Victory will be ours when we follow his pattern. When we get serious with God, we can say no to our fleshly appetites so that our spirits can gain strength.

I believe fasting will become a common practice again because of its importance: It's the part we play as the ground forces in God's battle plan. Angels may be God's air force, but the church is His army, and our fervent prayers open the windows of heaven. As James said, the 'effectual fervent prayer' of the righteous avails much (James 5:16).

What did Daniel's prayer and fasting set in motion? In response, God sent Daniel His answer: heavenly hosts to the rescue. The angel said he had been dispatched the minute the prayer – the fervent prayer – had started. You might say that Daniel started the battle by praying, pleading with God.

The Lord sent an answer, and then Satan countered by sending an opposing force to interfere with God's plan. For 21 days the battle raged, out of Daniel's sight. So the battle against the evil forces, in this case the prince of Persia, was obviously not Daniel's. Dake's Study Bible gives an interesting comment here: 'All wars lost or won on earth are results of wars that are won or lost by the heavenly army.' The battles are fought in the heavenlies, between Satan's angels and God's angels, not down here.

As I meditated on this reality, I was struck with a new insight. 'God,' I asked, 'my victory doesn't depend on my beating up the devil?'

The Lord answered, 'No, your part is to fast and pray. Let your requests be made known, then let Me send My heavenly hosts to your rescue. Let Me send someone who is a match for those wicked spirits. You are no match for the devil.

'Believe and pray. Knock and it will open. Ask and you will receive. Pray, praise and receive.'

With faith that the answer was on its way, Daniel continued

to hound heaven, and his prayers reinforced the Lord's angelic hosts. As if adrenaline were being pumped through their systems, their strength was renewed. Fresh troops arrived on the heavenly battlefield because the ground force was covering the field with prayer and praise. Though the evil forces fought their hardest, they were powerless to stop the answer from getting through to Daniel.

The devil has had us fooled. He has made us think that we have to beat him up, bind him, get him in a pit and sit on him before we can have any victory. We must resist the devil, but the battle and victory aren't ours. The battle is the Lord's and the victory is already His.

Our misunderstanding of the way the battle is waged could be tied to a mistranslation of Matthew 16:19. In the King James Version, Jesus says, 'And I will give unto thee the keys of the kingdom of heaven: and whatsoever thou shalt bind on earth shall be bound in heaven: and whatsoever thou shalt loose on earth shall be loosed in heaven.'

But more accurately the verb tenses should be translated: 'Whatsoever thou shalt bind on earth shall be that which has already been bound in heaven: and whatsoever thou shalt loose on earth shall be that which has already been loosed in heaven.' We do not originate victory; we cannot accomplish what has already taken place.

God is always in the offensive position. Satan's forces are trying to sabotage and interfere with a victory that has already been won by Jesus Christ, the Son of the living God, who was stronger than death, Satan's most powerful weapon.

The war has been won; all we have to do is start praying that the answer gets through to us. We pray, and God says that the answer is coming. He calls some warriors, some stealth bombers, and tells them to go penetrate the principalities and powers of the darkness of this world to deliver His answer.

Never doubt that God's answer is on its way. Sometimes we wait out a long and fiery battle. But we are called to stand firm in our belief, to pray that the line of interference will be broken and to praise Him for His victory.

The Old Testament is full of accounts of heavenly battles. In 2 Chronicles 20, King Jehoshaphat and God's people faced several threatening armies. What did the king do? He called upon God and asked his people to fast and pray. God's answer was this: 'Be not afraid; ... the battle is not yours, but God's ... Ye shall not need to fight in this battle: ... stand ye still, and see the salvation of the Lord with you' (vv. 15–17).

With that answer, the people continued to worship and praise God for the victory. A choir singing 'Praise the Lord' led their march toward the enemy, which they found already defeated. God had caused the enemy armies to fight among themselves and destroy one another.

Another example is the story of Gideon. What a battle in the heavenlies must have raged at the sound of Gideon's 300 soldiers blowing trumpets, breaking clay pitchers and shouting, 'The sword of the Lord, and of Gideon!' (Judges 7:18). The result? The whole Midianite army panicked and killed one another.

Joshua's army marched around Jericho and gave a shout. City walls fell down and an enemy was defeated simply because God's people shouted a confirmation of the victory that had just been won in the heavenlies. God's answer broke through to His people.

God gives His angels charge over His children. According to Psalm 91, those angels bear us in their hands to keep us from dashing our feet against stones. The Lord says, 'I don't expect you to know how to miss the bumps in the road. I'll send My angels to carry you.'

Psalm 34:7 gives another promise: 'The angel of the Lord encampeth round about them that fear him, and delivereth them.' Those encamping, delivering angels outpower and outnumber the enemy's forces. When Satan fell like lightning from heaven, a third of the angelic host went with him (Rev. 12:4). That means the Lord's angelic forces outnumber Satan's two to one.

Long ago I memorized a verse that climaxes a wonderful Old Testament story of victory. The king of Syria had sent an army to find and capture the prophet Elisha. During the night the enemy surrounded the city, and in the morning Elisha's servant reported horses, chariots and soldiers everywhere. The servant panicked, but Elisha prayed that God would open the man's eyes. 'Fear not,' Elisha said in words I can never forget. 'For they that be with us are more than they that be with them' (2 Kings 6:16).

As Elisha prayed, the young man saw the situation as it really was: 'The mountain was full of horses and chariots of fire round about Elisha' (v. 17). They were the Lord's chariots, encamped around His praying prophet.

No Syrian laid a hand on Elisha that day, and no evil need befall you. Fast and pray. The answer is on its way.

9

Binding the Strongman

by Larry Lea

Larry Lea is the founding pastor of the Church on the Rock in Rockwall, Texas. He started the church as a prayer meeting of 13 persons in 1980, and he saw it grow to over 6,000. Larry lea is one of the foremost leaders of today's American prayer movement. He is approaching his goal of recruiting an army of 300,000 intercessors who are committed to pray that the kingdom of God will come to America. His book Could You Not Tarry One Hour? *(Creation House) is one of the books on prayer I most highly recommend. Larry conducts what he calls 'Breakthroughs' in major metropolitan areas such as Los Angeles and Miami and Chicago, Philadelphia, San Francisco and other places, calling together thousands of intercessors who will corporately pray against the strongholds over those cities.*

How does Lea see these strongholds and the strongmen who occupy them? In an important book, The Weapons of Your Warfare *(Creation House), he shares what he has learned in plain, pastoral language with personal illustrations and applications. He tells the fascinating story of how he himself came face-to-face with a principality sent by the enemy to prevent this new church and ministry from flourishing in Rockwall. Larry Lea believes that when this*

Excerpted from *Charisma & Christian Life* magazine, 600 Rinehart Road, Lake Mary, Florida 32746. © 1989, Strang Communications Company.

wicked spirit was dealt with the darkness was pushed back so that the glory of God could shine more strongly in Rockwall. He sees as a sign that this happened the fact that 3,400 people walked the aisles of the church in the next twelve months to accept Jesus as Lord and Savior or to join the church.

*   *   *   *   *

Jesus was controversial. Not just a little. Not just occasionally. He was thoroughly, persistently controversial throughout most of His ministry.

Folks today who think they will follow Jesus, say the things He said, and do the things He did without encountering opposition are in for a rude awakening. Jesus was controversial in His day, and we who express His life and His teachings will be controversial today as well. Jesus even said so. He said to His apostles, 'If they treat the master of the house as if he's the devil, how do you think they'll treat you?' (See John 13:16.)

Despite great miracles and teachings that stirred and convicted the crowds, Jesus was accused of:

- not paying His taxes.
- tricking and manipulating the people and using magic to work His miracles.
- being an illegitimate son.
- being a fraud, a liar and a cheat.
- casting out demons by the power of Beelzebub, the chief of the devils.

In Luke 11:14–26, we read that Jesus cast out a devil from a man who was unable to speak. As soon as the demon was gone, the dumb man spoke and the people marvelled. But a few scoffed, 'He is casting out devils by the name of the ruler of devils.'

The Bible says that Jesus knew their thoughts and responded to the critics: 'Every kingdom divided against itself is brought to destruction, and a house divided against a house falls. If Satan also is divided against himself, how will his kingdom stand? ... But if I cast out demons with the finger of God, surely the kingdom of God has come upon you' (Luke 11:17–20).

Jesus went on to give them this illustration: 'When a strong man, fully armed, guards his own palace, his goods are in peace. But when a stronger than he comes upon him and overcomes him, he takes from him all his armor in which he trusted, and divides his spoils. He who is not with Me is against Me, and he who does not gather with Me scatters' (Luke 11:21–23).

Jesus was speaking directly about the devil and the power of his demons. He elaborated His point: 'When an unclean spirit goes out of a man, he goes through dry places, seeking rest; and finding none, he says, 'I will return to my house from which I came.' And when he comes, he finds it swept and put in order. then he goes and takes with him seven other spirits more wicked than himself, and they enter, and dwell there, and the last state of that man is worse than the first' (Luke 11:24–26).

Today God is raising up a company of people who know what the score really is, where the action really is in God. They're aware that unclean spirits are roaming this earth, seeking places to dwell in order to destroy men and women. This emerging company will have listening ears for what the Holy Spirit is saying to the church today, and they'll answer His call to battle. They know that this battle is a battle in the spirit realm, and they are ready for combat.

The Bible teaches that 'though we walk in the flesh, we do not war according to the flesh ... the weapons of our warfare are not carnal, but mighty in God for the pulling down of strongholds, casting down arguments and every high thing that exalts itself against the knowledge of God, bringing every thought into captivity to the obedience of Christ' (2 Cor. 10:3–5).

In another place the apostle Paul calls this great struggle a wrestling match, but he makes it clear that we do not 'wrestle against flesh and blood, but against principalities, against powers, against the rulers of the darkness of this age, against spiritual hosts of wickedness in the heavenly places' (Eph. 6:12).

A war is going on for our nation today. A war is being fought for our metropolitan areas, our great cities across this land. There's a war raging for our churches, for our families, and for each of us personally.

It's a war in the spirit realm, and this is the challenge you face: The devil has sent messengers, strong principalities and powers, to stand against you and to keep you from being and doing all that God has called you to be and do. *So what will you do about it?*

Recently as I was flying into a major city in this nation, we began to descend through a smoggy cloud toward the airport. We could see the sun above, but as we descended into the cloud we couldn't see the ground below. While I was praying in the spirit during those final few minutes of our flight, I had a spiritual vision that paralleled my physical look at this city. In my spirit I saw a dark cloud over that city.

I said, 'Lord, what is that cloud?'

He spoke in my spirit, 'That is the strongman and his minions hovering.' Then He showed me that similar clouds of darkness were over every major city in our nation.

I cried out in my spirit, 'What shall we do? That cloud must be removed!'

The Lord answered, 'Son, that's what the three hundred thousand intercessors in America are all about.'

God called me several years ago to raise up three hundred thousand men and women who would pray daily and intercede for America. That's the heartbeat of my ministry as I go from city to city across this nation. And when the Lord spoke that into my spirit, I immediately had a vision of those three hundred thousand intercessors lifting up their hands to God.

As they lifted up their hands, they were poking holes in the cloud of darkness with their fingertips. I was reminded again of that verse of Scripture in Luke: '*But if I cast out demons with the finger of God*, surely the kingdom of God has come upon you' (Luke 11:20, italics added). As those intercessors raised their hands, and their fingers poked holes through the clouds of darkness, the sunlight and the glory of God streamed through.

Your hands today are the extended hands of Jesus. Your hands are the only hands He has today in this world. When you lift up your hands into the air and declare with your mouth that the North, South, East and West must give up what belongs to God, you dislodge the strongman from his place over us.

The sun doesn't know how to do anything but shine. It never turns off, though it's sometimes covered from our view by clouds. The same is true for the Son of God. He never stops shining, but His glory is sometimes hidden from our view by dark spiritual clouds. When the powers of darkness are forced to flee and the strongman is bound, then the kingdom of God shines through and the glory of the Lord is manifested on the earth.

What is the nature of this spiritual cloud that may over-shadow a city? It's a spirit of darkness that obscures the glory of God and covers up the kingdom of God with sin and strife.

Over many cities a spirit of religion reigns. That's the spirit that divides brother from brother and says, 'I'm a Baptist' – or some other denomination – 'and you're a Methodist so there's no fellowship between us.' Or 'I'm a charismatic and you're a Catholic so there's no love flowing between us.' Whatever denominations may be involved, this spirit insists on dividing the church. With the spirit of religion, dogma is more import-ant than Jesus. But when we resist this spirit, we must insist that everyone who names the name of Jesus Christ and holds that name as their only hope of salvation is our brother or sister.

Over some cities are spirits of avarice and greed. Over others are spirits of violence. Over still others are spirits of addiction. So the only thing that will change what is going on in our cities is an army of intercessors who will stand and raise their hands in prayer and praise to poke holes in the darkness.

When enough holes are poked in the darkness, what hap-pens? The cloud collapses. It evaporates. It ceases to be. Sun-shine explodes over the face of the earth. We sing it in our song of praise: 'Arise, shine, for the glory of the Lord is come!'

A number of years ago, shortly after I was converted and

began to preach, my friend Jerry and I conducted a revival in Prospect, Texas, a little town just a few miles north of Rockwall. In those days Jerry preached and I led the singing. When we entered a town, we would usually meet together after the first service to ask God to show us the enemy forces at work in that particular town or church. Then we'd come against those spirits and bind them.

We had only been saved and filled with the Holy Spirit a year or so, but we knew it was God's will that His light and power would come upon the people. We believed with all our hearts what I still believe today: It is not God's will that any should perish, but that all should come to know the Lord. (See 2 Pet. 3:9). We felt strongly that it was our responsibility as evangelists to tear apart the spiritual darkness so that God's light could shine with full force on the people who heard us preach and sing and testify of His greatness.

As Jerry and I were praying on Saturday of that particular revival week, the Lord revealed to us that a spirit of fear dominated that church. He showed us especially the great fear in the pastor's heart. We got down in a little back room of that church and began to bind the spirit of fear. We declared that a spirit of boldness and courage would come over the people and be released in that area.

Now in many Baptist church revivals the custom is for the evangelist and the pastor to go 'witnessing' in the afternoons and then to conduct services in the evening. On that Saturday I said to the pastor, 'Let's go witness to the roughest sinner in town.'

So he said, 'OK. Let's go see ol' Harold Bull.' Even his name sounded tough to me!

We drove over to Harold's house, and Jerry stayed in the car to pray as the pastor and I went to the door. Harold had just come from his tractor. He was probably only about six feet, four inches tall, but he *looked* at least seven feet tall to me as he stood there behind the screen door of his house. He was dirty and he had a mean look on his face. The chaw of tobacco in his mouth looked about the size of a baseball.

The pastor started to speak, but when he opened his mouth, his voice cracked. In a voice three notes too high he finally stammered out, 'Hello, Harold, we've come to talk to you about our revival meeting.'

Harold just stared him down. Never said a word. Just stared.

Now I had prayed with Jerry for about four hours that morning, so I was dangerous at that particular moment. I was so full of God I was ready to spit holy nails. Suddenly I heard myself saying, 'Harold, what we really came out here to say is this: Do you want to be saved?'

Harold nearly swallowed that tobacco. He turned to stare at me. I got him in an eye-to-eye look. In my mind's eye I could imagine him tearing through that screen door and ripping my little head right off my body. But in my physical eyes, I looked at him with the love of Jesus and I didn't back down. I didn't have any fear in my heart. I just kept looking at him.

Finally he said, 'Yeah, I want to be saved.'

I said, 'Then get out here on the front porch, Harold.' He came out from behind the door and stood on the porch with us. I said, 'Now bow your head and spit out that tobacco and be reverent because we're going to pray.'

He spit out his tobacco and bowed his head, and we prayed. And ol' Harold got saved that afternoon!

Then I said, 'Now Harold, if you really mean this, you'll come to church, you'll walk down the aisle of that church and you'll make a public confession of your faith before God and everyone.'

We had revival that night and a few folks got saved, but Harold wasn't there. On Sunday morning, we started the song service and Harold wasn't there. We sang one song, and then another, and then another – and still no Harold.

Then suddenly the back door opened in that little wooden church, and there stood Harold. He nearly filled the door frame, and as he walked forward, you could hear his big work boots on the wooden floor. It was suddenly as if we were filming an E.F. Hutton commercial. When Harold walked in and sat down, everyone's head turned, and the place got so quiet you could have heard a pin drop.

Harold sat down, and Jerry stood up to preach. When Jerry gave the invitation to come forward and accept Jesus Christ, Harold stood up, walked forward and publicly gave his heart to Jesus.

Word spread like wildfire through that town that ol' Harold Bull had gone forward and been saved. By that night the little church was packed out. People were standing along the side walls of the church because there were no more chairs and no more room in the pews.

That night Jerry and I decided to lay hands on the people, every one of them. We didn't know any better than to do that in a Baptist church. We had been to a meeting where the minister walked around and laid hands on the people and prayed for them, so we decided we'd do that, too. And let me tell you, that place came *alive* that night!

Now I am 100-percent convinced that our revival services would have never been successful in that town and in that church unless Jerry and I had first prayed and discerned the nature of the strongman over the church and the town and then prayed that God would defeat the strongman and release His kingdom. I don't believe Harold would have been saved or the lives of that community changed on that Sunday morning without intercessory prayer first pushing holes through the darkness that had bound that church in fear.

What will you do when you're hit by the devil? Will you back up and back down? Or will you stay in there and fight with all your might?

Taking What is Rightfully Yours

Now the enemy is not only coming at you to bind you up and to keep you from being and doing all that God desires for you. The enemy is also at work to keep you from having all that God desires for you.

Look at God's promise in Isaiah 43:4–7:

90

Since you were precious in My sight, you have been honored, and I have loved you; therefore I will give men for you, and people for your life. Fear not, for I am with you, I will bring your descendants from the east, and gather you from the west; I will say to the north, 'Give them up!' and to the south, 'Do not keep them back!' Bring My sons from afar, and My daughters from the ends of the earth – everyone who is called by My name, whom I have created for My glory; I have formed him, yes, I have made him.

'Since you were precious in My sight.' You are precious to the Lord. He paid the price of His Son, Jesus Christ, on the cross for you. You were purchased by the blood of Jesus. You are precious to God.

At the Church on the Rock, when we pray together that phrase of the Lord's prayer that says, 'Thy kingdom come, thy will be done, on earth as it is in heaven,' we stand and turn to the North and say, 'North, give up what belongs to this church.' Then we turn to the East and say, 'East, give up what belongs to this church.' We turn to the South and to the West and say the same thing. We want everything that God wants to give us. We cry, 'Give up, enemy, what belongs to us. Don't hold back, enemy, what is ours.'

Now this refers to everything that God wants us to have. It means resources and blessings for our individual lives. It means souls being saved in our churches because sinners are coming in and hearing the Word of God preached with power. It means resources coming to our churches. It means every miracle that we need coming our way.

As the Church on the Rock grew in numbers, the Lord revealed to me in my times of prayer that my primary job as a pastor was to break through the spiritual darkness over Rockwall and over the lives of those He wanted to bring into our congregation. I knew beyond any shadow of a doubt that great preaching wouldn't cause souls to be saved and the church to grow. Finely honed theology spelled out in precise statements wouldn't do it. No, only the tearing down of strongholds that were holding back the people from experiencing God in their lives would cause the church to grow.

So I went to the church building on Saturday nights to pray especially for the services the next day. Often I met others there, but on one particular Saturday night I was alone. The church auditorium was dark, with only one light on above the baptistry in front.

As I knelt there and cried aloud to the Lord, I broke through into a spiritual dimension that I don't know how to describe for you. I was in 'rarified air' spiritually speaking. When I declared to the North, South, East and West to give up what belongs to the Church on the Rock, I felt a presence in that auditorium that was unlike anything I had ever experienced. And it was *not* a holy presence.

I was kneeling with my eyes closed, and at that moment when I felt this presence in the room, I looked up and in my spiritual vision I saw a being standing in front of me. He was holding a large silver chain in his hands. I'll never forget it as long as I live.

My first impulse was to get up and run out of the building. But at the same time, I knew that I was at a moment of truth, a divine intersection. I realized that I was face-to-face with the very power that was holding back the harvest of souls that God wanted to bring into the Church on the Rock.

The being communicated to me these words, 'Do you really mean it? Are you serious? Are you really going to take your stand?'

Immediately that inner Man within me – the One the Scriptures refer to as 'greater ... than he that is in the world' – stood up. Before I knew what I was doing, I literally stood to my feet and shouted back at this being, 'You're mighty right I mean what I'm saying!'

I stepped toward him, and when I did, he stepped back. I knew I had him on the run. He dropped the chain and disappeared. He was gone.

From that day to this, I have never encountered anything like that again. But in the next twelve months, we saw some thirty-four hundred people walk the aisles of the Church on the Rock getting saved or united with our church. We held no special revivals. We conducted no house-to-house canvasses. We sponsored no special membership drives. It happened solely by the power of God shining through the powers of darkness. The strongman had been bound and the kingdom of God released.

Something new is emerging in the spirit realm today. God is calling His church to rise up and become militant warriors who will stand and say to principalities and powers, 'Yes, we are taking a stand. Yes, we mean it. Yes, we declare to you that you will not have our children; you will not have our families; you will not have our churches; you will not have our blessings.' And we will drive back the darkness so that the glory of God might shine more strongly.

God's desire is for you to pray this way. Believe it!

What's the purpose of prayer anyway? Prayer is not coming to God to convince Him to do something He doesn't want to do. Prayer is coming into agreement with God about something He already wants to do. It's saying, 'I'll do my part so that You, Lord, are free to do Your part.'

God's desire is that you have all He wants you to have and experience all He wants you to experience for your spiritual good. Sometimes we don't think big enough. Sometimes we don't expect enough. Sometimes we don't desire His blessings nearly to the extent that He wants to give them.

I remember one time when I was praying and calling out to the North, South, East and West. God spoke in my spirit and said, 'You're turning to the North, but in your spirit you're only getting as far as Denton. And when you turn to the East, you're believing only as far as Greenville out in east Texas. Son, I'm the God of the whole world. When I turn to the East, I'm looking as far as *Germany*!'

The very next Sunday, I gave an invitation to people to join the church, and down the aisle walked a beautiful couple with their children. The Lord prompted me to stop them and ask them where they were from. The father stopped, clicked his heals, saluted me and said, 'My name is Lieutenant Bob Cooper, and I was stationed in Germany when I got your tapes on prayer. God told me to resign my commission in the military, which I've had for nine years, and move to Rockwall to report for duty.'

My soul nearly soared out of my body when that man said 'Germany.' I knew that I was standing in the heart of something very big. God has vast blessings for His people – there are no limits. But we must break through the darkness to let the kingdom come shining through. When you break through the spiritual powers and the glory of God starts to shine through, you don't have to do much preaching to get folks saved.

We had a musical at our church recently and the choir and orchestra were magnificent. But the greatest part of the service was watching some eighty people walk the aisle to accept Jesus Christ into their lives. My wife and I have grown up around great musicals all our lives. But most of the time, we've noticed that after a great evening performance by the choir, everybody 'oohs' and 'aahs' a bit, then they all fall silent while the pastor stands and leads the singing of 'Just As I Am.' Maybe one or two come forward at the most.

Our musical wasn't technically any better than those performed at most other places. The difference was that the choir was singing with the sun shining on them from heaven. The spiritual darkness had been punctured so that the glory of God could come through. Those who had prayed and interceded before God, not just that day, but every day at sunrise for year after year, had cleared the space. They had pushed back the powers of evil so that the kingdom of God might be established. And it was! Without a great effort. Without singing 'Just As I Am' ten times through. Without pleading. Eighty people accepted Jesus as Savior and Lord that one night. Now that's the kind of miracle that happens when the enemy is forced, by our taking a stand in prayer, to give up what belongs to God almighty.

We are to stand strong in the honor, love and courage of God and cry out, 'Give up, enemies to the North, everything

God has for me, for my family, for my church. Give up, enemies of the South, everything God has for me, for my family, for my church. Give up, enemies of the East, everything God has for me, for my family, and for my church. Give up, enemies of the West, everything God has for me, for my family and for my church. Give it up! It's mine! It's ours!'

God says, 'I'll do it. If you'll speak to the enemy like that, I'll do My part. I'll cause things to come your way. It will happen.'

When you declare these things, believe that they are done on earth as they are in heaven. When you start to fight battles like that, winning them for the Lord, though the world situation gets darker and darker, you'll shine brighter and brighter. As those in the world feel worse and worse, you'll be feeling better and better. As the world's systems get weaker and weaker, you'll grow stronger and stronger. As the world starts winding down, you'll be winding up. Instead of wondering what will happen next, you'll be asking, 'Where's the next victory, Lord?'

Give God the glory, for the great works He has done, is doing and will do. The victory is ours. It's yours. It's mine. It's a sure victory if we'll but fight the fight.

10

Jericho: Key to Conquest

by Dick Bernal

Dick Bernal is a preaching pastor and his pulpit fervor shows clearly in this fast-moving chapter. The founding pastor of Jubilee Christian Center in San Jose, California, Bernal leads a church of over 5,000 members in which blacks and whites, Hispanics and Asians, rich and poor joyously worship together. For the past several years teams from Jubilee have been systematically interceding for their city with some palpable results. In this chapter, using Jericho as a model, Dick Bernal concludes with nine practical principles for praying for your city.

The forty years the children of Israel spent wandering in the wilderness was not a total loss. God was making soldiers out of slaves, a task He is still undertaking today with all of His delivered ones. It didn't take long to get His people out of Egypt, but it took years to get Egypt out of His people!

Finally, the Lord was ready to send them into the promised land, a land of blessing and provision, but also a land with many challenges, the first being a mighty walled city, the city of Jericho.

Excerpted from *Come Down Dark Prince* by Dick Bernal © 1989, Companion Press, Box 351, Schippensburg, PA 17257 by permission of the author.

The First Encounter

Some have concluded that Joshua erred in sending the two
spies into Jericho to get a layout of the land. The critics
maintain that Joshua should have trusted wholly in the Lord
and not followed the example of Moses which led to an evil
report from the ten spies, with only Joshua and Caleb standing
in faith. Let me remind you, however, that it was God's idea to
spy out the land, not Moses'!

> And the Lord spoke to Moses, saying, 'Send men to spy
> out the land of Canaan, which I am giving to the children
> of Israel; from each tribe of their fathers you shall send a
> man, every one a leader among them' (Num. 13:1–2).

We should also remember that Joshua was one of the spies
and apparently saw merit in 'looking before one leaps'!

> Now Joshua the son of Nun sent out two men from Acacia
> Grove to spy secretly, saying, 'Go, view the land, espe-
> cially Jericho.' So they went, and came to the house of the
> harlot named Rahab, and lodged there (Josh. 2:1).

In Sodom and Gomorrah's case, intercession and 'drawing
near to God in the spirit' worked wonders and nearly saved two
rotten-to-the-core cities. Lot and his family were rescued.
Although Lot's wife's deliverance was short-lived, God still
honored Abraham's request.

But prayer alone is not enough. It is the beginning of city-
taking. It is preparing and planning in the Spirit, getting the
mind and strategy of Christ on just how to penetrate a city with
the gospel.

Spying out the land is essential when warring for a city. Most
Christians know how to get from their home to church, to the
store, to the malls, or to a friend's house. But how many really
know their city? Christians should walk or drive every major
freeway, avenue and road of their cities, praying and coming
against demonic strongholds over every neighborhood.

I have had the privilege of being raised in San José and have watched this sleepy little agricultural town explode into the heart of Silicon Valley. I have this city in my heart. I know it! I know its people! I have my hand on the pulse of it, monitoring each beat. I am constantly keeping surveillance over changes which affect its flow. Make no mistake, knowing your city is a necessary first step in taking your city for Christ.

When you move in faith to take your city for the Lord, two things will be true. First, the resistance you will experience is like nothing you've ever come up against before. When you tell the prince over your city, 'We're here to take it for God,' he will not just play dead; he will violently oppose you! That is why the Lord told Joshua over and over again, 'Be strong and of good courage; do not be afraid, nor be dismayed, for the Lord your God is with you wherever you go' (Josh. 1:9).

But, second, it's amazing who will come to your aid to help you win your city. Imagine a prostitute named Rahab as a key player in conquering Jericho! And what about David's feisty four hundred, 'those in distress, everyone who was in debt, and everyone who was discontented ... So he became captain over them' (1 Sam. 22:2). Out of David's 'maladjusted malcontents' came mighty men who knew how to possess the land promised to them.

Once the city had been surveyed and the scouting party had safely returned, the task of crossing the Jordan and actually taking the city had to be undertaken. Remember, Moses and the old school had died off. A new, younger generation stood at the Jordan. I'm finding out that it is this new, fearless generation today that is willing to take on a whole city.

> Then Joshua rose early in the morning; and they set out from Acacia Grove and came to the Jordan, he and all the children of Israel, and lodged there before they crossed over. So it was, after three days, that the officers went through the camp; and they commanded the people saying, 'When you see the ark of the covenant of the Lord your God, and the priests, the Levites, bearing it, then you

shall set out from your place and go after it. Yet there shall
be a space between you and it, about two thousand cubits
by measure. Do not come near it, that you may know the
way by which you must go, for you have not passed this
way before.' And Joshua said to the people, 'Sanctify
yourselves for tomorrow the Lord will do wonders among
you' (Josh. 3:1–5).

The ark here prefigured Christ as the believer's covenant
Guide. The contents of the ark represented the Word, the
authority and the provision of the Lord, capped off by a mercy
seat. 'Let it (the ark) go before you' was the command and 'you
go after it.'

To get ahead of God when trying to win a city could be fatal
to a church or a group of churches or a pastor, and even to the
sheep. I've noticed in some areas of the world where revival has
broken out that there is a high toll of casualties – divorce,
sickness, church splits, even death. A price too high to pay for
being impetuous.

Before the Lord had Joshua move on Jericho, the nation
participated in acts of committal: The erecting of memorial
stones (Josh. 4), and the circumcision of all males who hadn't
been circumcised in the wilderness (Josh. 5).

In ancient times, altars of stone were erected as reminders of
some wonderful intervention by God, as memorials to remind
coming generations of God's goodness and power toward His
people.

The Lord is about to deliver a whole city into the hands of
His people Israel, but knowing how prone human hearts are to
forget His past interventions, He demanded an altar of
remembrance. A passage of Scripture recurring too often in
the Old Testament is 'They soon forgot His works' (Ps.
106:13).

The Lord held back the waters of the Jordan as a sign and
wonder to the heathen and as a reminder to His people that the
same God who parted the Red Sea some forty years earlier for
Moses was indeed with Joshua in battle. The twelve stones

were taken from the bottom of Jordan. Smooth stones, shaped and constantly cleansed by a moving river. These twelve stones represented each tribe, showing God's love and interest not simply in the masses but in individuals. These city-takers had a God who knew them, loved them, would fight for them; a God who took the rough edges off them by a rushing flow of His Spirit.

Before God could turn them loose on Jericho, some important unfinished business needed to be attended to – circumcision! The 'circumcising of the sons of Israel again the second time,' needs a word of explanation. Obviously, the Scriptures are not suggesting these men needed to be circumcised again, any more than you and I need to be 'born again' again! Knowing the importance of circumcision as the token or sign of the covenant with God (Gen. 17:9–11), it is inconceivable that this was a slight oversight on behalf of the children of Israel. Another question arises: How come Moses didn't put his foot down and demand that all males who were born in the wilderness be circumcised? Scholars and commentators have argued over this point for years. Some say, 'Sinful neglect.' Others suggest, 'Because of their frequent journeying and the inconvenience of performing circumcision, they kept putting it off.'

Matthew Henry concedes the explanation is found in Numbers 14. 'Because of their infidelity and evil hearts, they tasted the breach of His promise; their apostasy and breaking of the covenant releasing Him from His engagement to bring them into Canaan.' Circumcision is a type of the mortification of sin and the putting off of the filth of the flesh.

City-takers are going to stir up the enemy's nest. Only the cleansed and sanctified will be victorious in battle. I'm not talking about the hyper-holy, super-do-gooders, but about those who know their God and who do great exploits (Dan. 11:32).

The City Itself

A key city! A powerful fortress of seemingly impregnable walls! An invisible sign seems to say, 'God's people, listen up. You shall go no further. Stop!' If Jericho could be taken, what encouragement it would bring to the children of Israel and what a message it would send to the other cities of Canaan! Think of it! It would be like taking New York, Miami, or Los Angeles, even San Francisco. What a blow to Satan's kingdom! But what joy it would bring to the camp of the redeemed!

Our attitude toward winning a city has been basically to gather at the church for a prayer meeting and bind the devil until we're blue in the face. I believe there is an active side to warfare as well as a passive one. As an old sage once said, 'It's time to vitalize the legal.' In other words, put feet to our covenant rights and promises.

Only after the Hebrew nation had built a memorial altar, had been circumcised and had kept the Passover, was it time for them to move on the city.

> And Joshua rose early in the morning, and the priests took up the ark of the Lord. Then seven priests bearing seven trumpets of rams' horns before the ark of the Lord went on continually and blew with the trumpets. And the armed men went before them. But the rear guard came after the ark of the Lord, while the priests continued blowing the trumpets. And the second day they marched around the city once and returned to the camp. So they did six days. But it came to pass on the seventh day that they rose early, about the dawning of the day, and marched around the city seven times in the same manner. On that day only they marched around the city seven times. And the seventh time it was so, when the priests blew the trumpets, that Joshua said to the people: 'SHOUT FOR THE LORD HAS GIVEN YOU THE CITY!' (Josh. 6:12–16).

This was far more than human conflict. Jehovah God Himself was waging war against Satan and his hosts! The Canaanites were devoted to idolatry, divination, necromancy, witchcraft, charms and familiar spirits. The children of Israel would be the instruments of God's judgment upon these wicked, perverted people.

When you come into the land which the Lord your God is giving you, you shall not learn to follow the abominations of those nations. There shall not be found among you anyone who makes his son or his daughter pass through the fire, or one who practices witchcraft, or a soothsayer, or one who interprets omens, or a sorcerer, or one who conjures spells, or a medium, or a spiritist, or one who calls up the dead. For all who do these things are an abomination to the Lord, and because of these abominations the Lord your God drives them out from before you. You shall be blameless before the Lord your God. For these nations which you will dispossess listened to soothsayers and diviners; but as for you, the Lord your God has not appointed such for you' (Deut. 18:9–14).

These satanic strongholds had to be pulled down, and according to Paul we must do the same.

But I say that the things which the Gentiles sacrifice they sacrifice to demons and not to God, and I do not want you to have fellowship with demons. You cannot drink the cup of the Lord and the cup of demons; you cannot partake of the Lord's table and of the table of demons (1 Cor. 10:20–21).

A key verse to focus on in this whole process of spiritual warfare is verse 2 of Joshua 6:

And the Lord said to Joshua: 'See, I have given Jericho into your hands, its king, and the mighty men of valor.'

Immediately we see who gets the credit for the victory. 'God resists the proud, but gives grace to the humble' (Jas. 4:6).

The Game Plan

A.W. Pink brings up a good point: 'If the Lord has definitely given Jericho into the hands of Joshua, why were such elaborate preparations as these necessary for its overthrow?' (*Gleanings from Joshua*, p. 149).

Pink answers his own question.

> Let those who feel the force of any such difficulty weigh attentively what we are about to say. In reality, those verses exemplify and illustrate a principle which it is most important for us to apprehend. That principle may be stated thus: the disclosure of God's gracious purpose and the absolute certainty of its accomplishment in no wise renders needless the discharge of our responsibilities. God's assuring us of the sureness of the end does not set aside the indispensability of the use of means. Thus, here again, as everywhere, we see preserved the balance of Truth.

God's promises should never promote inactivity on our part. Many pastors who have read my book, *Storming Hell's Brazen Gates*, have told me, 'God has given us our city,' yet few have ever shared God's instructions and strategy for conquest with me. One man of God and a dear friend, Ed Silvoso, is an exception.

Ed, the brother-in-law of Luis Palau and Juan Carlos Ortiz, is, like these great preachers, an Argentine. Ed is a thinker, a strategist. He and his team from Harvest Evangelism, a ministry over which he presides, has targeted a city in Northern Argentina. Their street-by-street, block-by-block attack on the ruling princes, followed up with crusades, Bible studies, concerts and personal evangelism is very exciting to me. I wish I were right in the middle of it! Their main focus, once the rest has taken place, is church planting.

How strange God's instructions must have sounded to Joshua. Can you imagine the look on the faces of the men in his army when he shared the battle plan! There have been more than a few eyebrows raised over some of my teaching on dethroning the prince over San Jose, California.

Once again, please note the importance of the ark. God's

presence was with them as they marched. This was not going to be a victory brought about by the arm of the flesh but by 'His Spirit.'

And then, the blowing of the trumpets. The Bible has much to say about the significance of the trumpet's blast. We are told to lift up our voices like a trumpet, to sound the alarm, to hearken to its sound, just to name a few.

At Jericho, I'm sure it was used to frighten the enemy as well as to encourage the Israelites. I know beyond a shadow of a doubt that when our church gathers for praise and worship and our band 'gets it going' with the brass section wailing away and the saints entering into the high praises of God, the demons shudder and become confused while the children of God are refreshed and strengthened.

The seventh verse of Joshua 6 is very powerful. It isn't just the priests doing the marching or warfare, but also the rank and file. Today we have too many worn-out preachers trying to go it alone. No one shows up at the prayer meetings or joins in a called fast; so the preacher tries it solo. No, that's not God's way. The pattern we see at Jericho is of the priests blowing the trumpet and the people marching. What harmony!

Notice another interesting aspect of their strategy in Joshua 6:10, 11:

> Now Joshua had commanded the people, saying, 'You shall not shout or make any noise with your voice, nor shall any word proceed out of your mouth, until the day I say to you, 'Shout!' Then you shall shout.' So he had the ark of the Lord circle the city, going around it once. Then they came into the camp and lodged in the camp.

This was no time for personal opinion, preaching, murmuring, war cries or goofing off. Just holy, orderly silence. The first day must have seemed like a waste of time and energy to some. Yet much was accomplished. They were obedient to God's every instruction! No one added to or took away from God's plan. 'Has the Lord as great delight in burnt offerings and sacrifices, as in obeying the voice of the Lord? Behold, to obey is better than sacrifice ... ' (1 Sam. 15:22).

Further, in making the Israelites march around the city once each day for six days and seven times on the seventh day, it is obvious that the Lord was teaching His people not only obedience, but patience and timing. I've often wondered what was going on in the minds of the inhabitants of Jericho. Was God lulling them to sleep with a false sense of security? What would you think if all your enemies ever did was silently march around your fortress?

> But it came to pass on the seventh day that they rose early, about the dawning of the day, and marched around the city seven times in the same manner. On that day only they marched around the city seven times. And the seventh time it was so, when the priests blew the trumpets, that Joshua said to the people: 'Shout, for the Lord has given you the city!' (Josh. 6:15–16).

This was no ordinary shout! It had been bottled up in them for six days, faith and absolute obedience wanting desperately to express itself in victory. 'By faith the walls of Jericho fell down after they were encircled for seven days' (Heb. 11:30). How much of our shouting at our city walls and gates is noise and not faith?

> So the people shouted when the priests blew the trumpets. And it happened when the people heard the sound of the trumpet, and the people shouted with a great shout, that the wall fell down flat. Then the people went up into the city, every man straight before him, and they took the city (Josh. 6:20).

Then, and only then, was victory theirs for the taking. It was the culmination of a process of warfare involving commitment, cleansing and unconditional obedience. Let's summarize and glean a few truths from the taking of Jericho to apply in taking our own cities for God:

1) No city is too tough for God.
2) Gaze on your city through the eyes of faith.
3) Even though it is God who is doing the fighting, we still have our responsibilities.
4) Stay humble.
5) Use His Word and stay in His presence.
6) Survey the territory.
7) Stick to God's plan.
8) Even if you don't see instant results, keep the trumpets blowing.
9) Always remember, God is not slack concerning His promise; the walls will come down!

11

Prayer Power in Argentina

by Edgardo Silvoso

Edgardo Silvoso, a native-born Argentine, is the founding president of Harvest Evangelism, a ministry dedicated to the evangelization of Argentina and based in San Jose, California. Through the years Silvoso has observed the effectiveness of power evangelism in the urban centers of his nation. In this brief chapter, which introduces some of Argentina's most effective evangelists and pastors, Silvoso describes several field case studies of the use of strategic level intercession which apparently has been successful in pushing back the principalities and powers, allowing the light of the gospel to shine through more brightly.

*   *   *   *   *

Argentina has consistently produced top quality pastors, evangelists and theologians. Men like Luis Palau, Juan Carlos Ortiz, Alberto Mottessi and Samuel Libert have blessed the body of Christ worldwide. All of them would readily credit the church in Argentina with the reasons for their success. However, that same church has had the lowest rate of church

From *Global Church Growth*, July–September 1987, © 1987 The Church Growth Center of Corunna, Indiana, used by permission of the author.

growth among all the nations in Latin America, with the probable exception of Uruguay. Until not too long ago, the average church in Argentina had less than 100 members. The lack of growth has puzzled experts, especially in the context of a church that is consistently capable of producing top quality international leaders but somehow fails to translate that ability into local church growth.

All of that has changed lately. C. Peter Wagner has stated that Argentina, along with mainland China, is 'the' flashpoint for church growth in the world today. No hard figures are available, but churches that used to have fifty members have grown to 1,000. Several churches have more than 5,000 people. There exists what Wagner calls a centrifuge church. Ministers go to the people by holding meetings in over fifty different locations rather than expecting the people to come to one place. The centrifuge church, Vision of the Future, ministers to 90,000 members. Hector Gimenez, a lay preacher, was able to plant a church of 20,000 members in downtown Buenos Aires in less than six months. Carlos Annacondia, Argentina's leading lay evangelist, has led over one million people to a decision for Christ in less than four years. Yet, he is not the only one. There are at least a dozen evangelists and hundreds of younger preachers with the same degree of zeal who are efficiently preaching in every corner of the nation.

The church in Argentina has grown more in the last four years than in the previous one hundred. Norberto Carlini, pastor of the largest congregation in Rosario, had to move his congregation out of the building onto an open field in anticipation of growth. In less than three years, the church grew from several hundred to almost 5,000. Pastor Alberto Scataglini, in the city of La Plata, used to minister to 400 people a month. When the revival broke out, that figure jumped to several thousands. And more growth is anticipated. Many churches are moving out of conventional buildings that were designed to hold a few hundred at the most, into basketball stadiums, open fields and convention centers. It is not uncommon to find 'house-churches' meeting in backyards with three to four hundred members under the leadership of young pastors or somebody in his early twenties who has not been a Christian for more than three years.

The Baptist church in downtown Buenos Aires, under the leadership of Pastor Pablo Deiros, grew 43% in 1986 and 65% in the first six months of 1987. Other churches are growing so fast that figures are not available because they drastically change from week to week. Pastor Regge, in Olivos, a plush community north of Buenos Aires, according to an article published in 'El Puente', leads a multicampus congregation estimated at 70,000 members. When asked what is the current membership, he shrugs his shoulders and says: 'It is hard to say. One of our annexes (sort of a daughter church) that is led by an ex-nun has over 6,000 people.' And that is jut an annex!

This is quite a change from the stagnant growth of only five years ago. What is the reason behind this explosion? There is a combination of factors. The unity of the body of Christ is partly due to the establishment of A.C.I.E.R.A., an organization that brings together the majority of denominations in Argentina. The emerging of the Pentecostal Federation of Argentina has provided the Pentecostal churches with visible unity and the ability to maximize resources. The ministry of the '700' club and its close work with local churches all over Argentina, has undoubtedly helped. I am sure that there are many other factors, but I would like to single out what key leaders consider to be the most important: prayer. The church in Argentina has learned to pray.

It is not uncommon for churches to hold all night prayer meetings, especially on the eve of a national holiday. I visited one of those and 13,000 attended! Some churches have the custom of holding prayer meetings that begin on Friday evening and go on until Sunday morning. Pastor Scataglini's church in La Plata, where the revival began in January of 1983, holds prayer meetings in the basement after every service. Hundreds of young people spend most of the night in prayer, and they enjoy it tremendously! Omar Cabrera, pastor of the 'centrifuge' church of 90,000 has trained his people to carry a

111

prayer book with them at all times. As prayer needs arise, they jot them down in their books and pray for them until the Lord answers. Pastor Guillermo Prein, leader of a fast growing congregation in Buenos Aires, told me: 'If I call the people to a business or teaching meeting, some will come. But if I invite them to a prayer meeting, all of them will come!'

Carlos Annacondia, who leads an average of 1,000 people a day to a public commitment to Christ, has patterned his crusade ministry around four 'times' of prayer. First he preaches to the unsaved and ends with a rich time of prayer for and with the new converts. People go away with the certainty that they have spoken to God. After a musical break comes a time of spiritual warfare prayer in which Carlos prays for those who are demonized. As he leads in prayer, hundreds, sometimes up to one thousand, fall to the ground under demonic oppression. They are carried by co-workers to a huge tent behind his platform – called 'The Intensive Care Unit' – where they are ministered to in prayer for several hours until deliverance comes. After another break, he prays for the sick. Finally, he prays for everybody who wants to be filled with the Holy Spirit by laying hands on them. I have estimated that of the two hours that Annacondia spends on the platform ministering, over one hour is actually spent in prayer. Under the platform he has a 'prayer brigade' of approximately fifty people who, for the duration of the meeting (sometimes up to seven hours) are in prayer.

Hector Gimenez, the layman who leads the largest church in downtown Buenos Aires, has built his ministry around prayer. People come to his meetings to pray and to be prayed for. The moment of prayer is the highlight of the service. Omar Cabrera regularly instructs his people to begin praying as they come into the meetings. I attended one of those meetings in which 24,000 packed a soccer stadium. It was inspiring to see the majority of the people taking spiritual possession of the stadium as they arrived. The Baptist church in Adrogue, under the leadership of Eduardo Lorenzo, keeps records of every major answer to prayer in a 'miracle book.' Samuel Libert's church in Rosario, another Baptist church, is known for its emphasis on prayer and body life. It is not uncommon to see believers in buses, parks, and even restaurants, praying together. As they meet socially, it is customary to end the evening with a time of prayer. And when prayer time comes around, it is not only the adults that pray but also children. One of the most moving pictures I have of Argentina is to see children, as small as six years old, on their knees praying!

All kinds of prayers are offered in Argentina, but the most unique prayer is in the context of spiritual warfare. Christians seem to have two focuses in their prayers: God, to whom they address all honor and praise; and, Satan, whom they boldly and aggressively rebuke. Believers subscribe to the view that prayer plays a vital active role in God's plan of redemption. They claim that without the church's prayer God will not retake the territory invaded by Satan. They are quick to point out that every verse in the Bible dealing with prayer indicates that the action begins on earth. We must ask for Him to answer. We must knock for Him to open. We must bind and release for heaven to do the same. The action on earth not only precedes but to some extent determines the answer in heaven. When it comes to preaching the gospel, it is the church's responsibility to cast out demons, to heal the sick and to tread over the power of the enemy.

This approach has made prayer exciting. When people pray they expect something to happen. They engage the enemy and they bind him. And then they move on and loot his camp. Omar Cabrera, considered by some the dean of power evangelism in Argentina, consistently closets himself in a hotel room for five to seven days of aggressive prayer before opening up a new city. During that time, he prays for binding of the strong man, or prince, who controls the darkness of that particular 'cosmos.' Once he feels that this has been accomplished, he goes public announcing to the people that now they are free to come to Christ. Like prisoners freed from a dungeon, thousands literally run to give their hearts to Christ.

Carlos Annacondia begins his crusades by showing the

pastors how to take control over the area. The night before the beginning of a crusade, all workers participate in a prayer meeting so intense that it reminds one of Joshua and the people marching around Jericho. When Annacondia went to the city of Cordoba, Argentina's most sophisticated center, many predicted that he would fail. Carlos' approach paid off again. Fifty-eight thousand made a commitment to Christ in two months!

Floro Olivera, pastor of a Brethren church in San Justo, a suburb of Buenos Aires, and his elders decided to put a specific section of their town under spiritual authority. In a very short time they saw massive conversions coming out of that area. Today they have moved out of the church building and onto the backyard of a school next door, due to dramatic growth in membership.

Eduardo Lorenzo and his fellow leaders at the Baptist church in Adrogue have been battling with a prince of darkness who controls the entire county where the church sits. They have already begun to see dramatic results not only in their own church but in the rest of the county as well.

The reasoning behind this approach lies in the assumption that God's power is somehow limited by God's moral character. When God created the world He entrusted it to Adam, who lost it to Satan. At that point in time Satan became the 'god of this world,' and the kingdoms of this world and their glory became his possession. Even though God could retake the world easily, his power is limited by moral law. Satan could accuse God of trespassing if He were to intervene directly. Since the government of earth was lost by Adam, a man, only another man could recover it. But since all men have sinned, they are automatically under Satan's dominion. However, God solved the problem through the incarnation of Christ. By being conceived by the Holy Spirit, He is divine and the evil one has no claim on Him. By being born of the virgin Mary, He is a bonafide member of the human race. That is why – the reasoning goes – when Jesus defeated Satan, first in the wilderness and later at Calvary and the resurrection as the second Adam,

He was able to take away from Satan, in a potential sense, what Satan had stolen from the first Adam. Every time the church (as the representative of the second Adam) prays, it provides the legal and moral justification for God to release his power. And that is why the prayers of the saints are so important.

Whether or not one fully agrees with this reasoning, it must be conceded that it does make praying an exciting exercise. It makes the believer not only a participant but also a partner in carrying out the Great Commission. And when it comes to prayer, the difference is as big as the satisfaction found in swimming in the bathtub as opposed to the ocean. By enlarging the perimeters and allowing for uncharted currents to bear on the swimmer, prayer becomes exciting. By seeing thousands come out of darkness in direct answer to prayer, faith is strengthened. By witnessing miracles immediately after a prayer meeting, the Word of God is validated and so are the promises it contains. After a while, people naturally gravitate toward prayer for the same reason that plants follow the sun: because from the sun they get the benefit of its power and greatness.

12

City Taking in Korea

by Paul Yonggi Cho

Although it is quite short, this chapter is worth reading because it was written by Paul Yonggi Cho, pastor of the world's largest church. Whenever he tells the story of how the Yoido Full Gospel Church grew to over 600,000 members, he emphasizes first and foremost the spiritual dynamics of the ministry. Here Cho stresses how important prayer, sacrifice and holiness are in taking a city for God.

We are living upon the threshold of a historical landmark in the church age. For this reason, I have always considered myself extremely fortunate to be able to serve God in these critical times. In these last days, God is moving mightily by His Spirit and is commanding us to arise, to cross over, to engage in battle, and to possess the land. God is raising up a great army to accomplish His purposes in our generation.

My ministry started with city taking. When I first pioneered my church, nobody would come to our old, torn marine tent because there was great demonic oppression over the village. The key to breaking that bondage was the casting out of a demon from a woman who had lain paralyzed for seven years.

Excerpted from the Foreword to *Come Down Dark Prince* by Dick Bernal © 1989 Companion Press, Box 351, Schippensburg, PA 17257 by permission.

When, after months of prayer, the demon oppressing her was cast out and she was healed, our church exploded with growth. The sky above the village was broken open and the blessings of God began pouring down. Today, the Yoido Full Gospel Church is still growing. We are now in excess of 600,000 members and we are marching forward to our goal of one million members by the year 1992.

The growth of our church and the growth of Christianity throughout the nation of Korea did not come by accident. It came through fervent, violent, prevailing prayer. As Jesus said in Matthew 11:12, 'The kingdom of heaven suffers violence, and the violent take it by force.' For example, in our church we have all night prayer meetings every single evening where thousands come to pray. On Friday evenings, more than fifteen thousand people join hearts and hands to pray for the Kingdom of God to come. On Prayer Mountain, at least three thousand people are praying, fasting, and ministering unto the Lord on any given day. In all, one-and-a-half million people visit and pray there in any given year. This is not limited only to our church; all over South Korea Christians are praying. One of the most unique characteristics of the Korean church is that millions gather early every morning at 5:30 a.m. to pray, despite wind, rain or snow.

Great sacrifices were made by the Korean church. The Kingdom of God indeed suffered violence. There was a long history of persecuting Christians by the Communists, as well as by the Japanese occupation forces. For instance, the Japanese installed Shinto altars in all Christian churches. The military police stood guard to enforce the law that required all Christians to bow down to the Shinto altar before entering to worship Almighty God. Those who refused were jailed and punished severely, with many ministers being executed at the hands of the Japanese forces. Many churches corporately decided to oppose this injustice. Many such churches were locked, with women and children inside, and burned to the ground due to their refusal to worship idols. Until recently, it took great sacrifice to be a Christian in Korea. Believers were a minority. But now, because 'the blood of the martyrs is the seed of the church,' we count at least one-fourth of our nation to be believers in the Lord Jesus Christ.

Finally, a word of admonition. It is so necessary for those who are called to engage in this spiritual warfare to be holy and sanctified, because He is a holy God. Many who have cast out demons, who have prophesied, and who have done wonders in His Name may find God declaring, 'Depart from me you who practise lawlessness, I never knew you.' The devil has crept into the Church and promoted iniquity, lawlessness and unrighteousness in our midst.

It breaks my heart to see so many co-workers for the Kingdom falling in disgrace. Like the seven sons of Sceva, the evil spirit leapt upon them, overpowered them, prevailed against them, and they fled out of their homes naked and wounded. Without holiness and sanctification, without great sacrifice, and without a fervent prayer life, many will be so wounded. The evil spirit will answer, 'Jesus I know, Paul I know, but who are you?'

It would do us well to be admonished by the great Apostle Paul:

> Finally, my brethren, be strong in the Lord and in the power of His might. Put on the whole armor of God, that you may be able to stand against the wiles of the devil. For we do not wrestle against flesh and blood, but against principalities, against powers, against the rulers of the darkness of this age, against spiritual hosts of wickedness in the heavenly places. Therefore, take up the whole armor of God, that you may be able to withstand in the evil day, and having done all, to stand. Stand, therefore, having girded your waist with truth, having put on the breastplate of righteousness, and having shod your feet with the preparation of the gospel of peace; above all, taking the shield of faith with which you will be able to quench all the fiery darts of the wicked one. And take the helmet of salvation, and the sword of the Spirit, which is the word of

God; praying always with all prayer and supplication in the Spirit, being watchful to this end with all perseverance and supplication for all the saints (Eph. 6:10-18).

13

High Level Powers in Zimbabwe

by Richmond Chiundiza

An increasing amount of information on territorial spirits is coming from Christian leaders in the Third World who have had knowledge of them for some time, but who have until recently been reticent about telling what they know. This has partly been due to an underlying fear that if they spoke about territorial spirits they would be written off by Western church leaders as flaky or unbalanced. Especially since the great Lausanne II Congress on World Evangelization held in Manila in 1989, Third World leaders have been more willing to dialogue on issues of spiritual warfare with Westerners. At Lausanne II five workshops were held on themes relating to territorial spirits, and the subject gained a degree of legitimacy it did not have previously.

The following interview is between Ted Olsen of Dawn Ministries and Richmond Chiundiza, national director of Disciples In Action Ministries, Zimbabwe. In 1982, Richmond Chiundiza started Glad Tidings Fellowship with six people. By 1990, he had 3000 members and had planted 25 other churches and started 5 preaching points. Chiundiza, who participated in the Manila congress, has researched extensively the spiritistic religion of the Shona people of Zimbabwe

---

in order to help free new believers from the strong control of their old religion and to see churches grow.

* * * * *

DAWN: When the Gospel was first proclaimed to the Shona in Zimbabwe over 100 years ago, there was the concept of a supreme being. His name was Mwari. Some missionaries and many church leaders today have contextualized the Christian message and Mwari became God. Has this been a good thing or not?

CHIUNDIZA: Even though the Shona religion is centered mostly on ancestral spirit worship, a study on the Shona concepts of God seems to reveal Mwari as God. Several of his names in the Shona language describe his character. *Muwanikwa* or *mutangakugara* mean 'he who existed before everything else;' *msiki* is 'creator of all things' and *wokumusorosoro* means the supreme, preeminent and transcendent God.

This basic understanding is in accordance with Romans 1:18–23 which shows God's revelation to men through conscience (v. 19) and creation (v. 20). However, the Shona understanding of God is inadequate. The devil has taken advantage of this 'inadequate revelation' by introducing the spirits as the center of worship. Consequently, the spirits have become a substitute for God.

DAWN: In Daniel 10, the angel comes to Daniel after a 21-day battle with the 'prince of the Persian kingdom.' This was a demonic ruler installed over a geographical region and working within the world system of Satan. We read in the same passage of a prince over Greece. Is there a prince over Zimbabwe?

CHIUNDIZA: Yes, I believe there are demonic princes set over Zimbabwe. My research is directed in part at discovering the identity of these princes. Zimbabwe is made up of two people groups – over seven million Shona and nearly two million Ndabele. From what I can discern, the highest ranking spirits over Zimbabwe are set over these two major people groups of the nation.

DAWN: Have you identified these high-ranking territorial spirits?

CHIUNDIZA: Yes, they have been identified.

There are two high-level powers in the heavenlies who can be said to be princes over the Shona people of Zimbabwe. They are Nehanda and Chaminuka. Both Nehanda and Chaminuka were people in history who died around the turn of the century. They became legends among the Shona because of their exploits. Demonic powers have inhabited the legends of Nehanda and Chaminuka and possess the bodies of a few key 'spokesmen' for the spirit world.

Nehanda, a Shona woman who took a stand against the colonial powers and was executed for her rebellion, is today the more powerful of the two princes. In many areas of Zimbabwe, the spirit powers of Nehanda are awesome.

Chaminuka was a man known as a prophet. He could foretell the future. One of his visions foretold the coming of the white men to Zimbabwe. Chaminuka's vision also included a rolling apparition which is interpreted as the arrival of the steam locomotive. His power in the spirit world is strong, and he is consulted even by government officials on certain occasions.

DAWN: If Nehanda and Chaminuka are the princes set over the demonic hierarchy, how do the familiar or ancestral spirits fit in?

CHIUNDIZA: Next in order to prominence are the Mondoro, or the demonic rulers set over the Shona clans who live in distinctly separate territories in Zimbabwe. The Mondoro inhabit the legends and identities of the founders of the Shona clans (a coalition of families).

In times of drought or calamity, the Shona go to communicate with these high ranking spirits. Year after year, these festivals take place at specific places such as the Great Zimbabwe ruins, a favorite spirit place for the Shona. It is a time of brewing beer which is offered to the spirits. Animal sacrifices are made and many rituals are undertaken. A person who is known to be possessed by the spirit of Nehanda or Chaminuka will speak the will of the high spirit.

A witch doctor, known as a N'anga, supervises the process of possession by the high spirit. Other people, possessed by the lesser spirits of the ancestors, must confirm this person is truly possessed by the high spirit.

The possessed person, who can be either a man or a woman, will remain possessed by this spirit until he does. Manifestation comes during these times of spiritistic consultation. The Mondoro control life within the clan territory and out of it. If a Shona leaves his traditional homeland he risks leaving the territorial guardianship of the spirits. He must first ask permission of the territorial spirit. This is done through an N'anga. In addition, he must wear a charm, such as a twig concealed in the hair or a bracelet worn under a sleeve, to carry the protective covering of the Mondoro with him. Many thousands in Zimbabwe who work in the cities give special attention to appeasing the territorial clan spirits each day and remaining under their protection.

Under the Mondoro, there are the Mudzimu. These are the lowest ranking of demons and are the ancestral or familiar spirits. They are believed to be the spirits of grandfathers, grandmothers, aunts and uncles. They are nonetheless important, and the Shona give much time and energy to appeasing them every day. Food sacrifices are a common form of appeasement.

DAWN: The Shona clans are ruled to this day by chiefs. How does the chief fit into this spiritistic system of control?

CHIUNDIZA: Almost every person in Zimbabwe is under the authority of a chief. And every chief is chosen by the clan spirits through a demonized spirit medium. So it is accurate to say that every person in Zimbabwe is traditionally under the control of the spirits.

The chief's main function is to be a steward to the spirits. He responds to their directives and controls over the people. When a chief is selected, the clan spirits, the Mondoro, come on a person recognized as a medium during a demonic seance.

The spirits literally select the next chief. He is pointed out by the possessed medium who knows the secrets of his life and the controls that other demons already have over him. This man, when he is chosen, knows that he owes his job, his income, his privileges, to the spirit for the rest of his life. This commitment will involve the whole clan.

The chief sees that all the traditions in keeping with the Mondoro are followed. The practical implications are obvious. Millions of Zimbabweans are under the direct control and authority of demons.

DAWN: Would a Zimbabwean who is now living in the city be expected to participate in this process of joining in with the clan to appease the spirits?

CHIUNDIZA: Yes. At least once a year – usually over a holiday such as Easter – everyone within the clan families receives word that they are expected to go home for a time of ritual appeasement. Anyone who fails to appear is seen as being in open rebellion. Such a one risks the vengeful reaction of the spirits, and these demonic punishments are very harsh and very real.

When someone is seen as having alienated the spirits there is subsequently the need for appeasement. This is not a cute cultural ritual. It is an unadulterated demonic practice. By far the majority of Zimbabwe's 10 million are involved in these practices and are under the authority of these Mondoro spirits.

DAWN: You've referred to the power of these spirits as being very real. How is this demonstrated?

CHIUNDIZA: When a spirit medium speaks under possession, he'll tell you exactly what has happened in your life in the past. He'll prophecy that certain things will happen to you in the future and these things happen, even down to the little details. You may be told that you'll get a job next week on Thursday – and you do. Or you'll hear that you're going to lose your hand in a machine accident at work during April, and it happens. People fear this kind of control. Healings take place, curses make people sick or die. The healings are very real. The curses often kill people.

The tragic problem is that the Shona people don't know from whom this power comes. The teaching on Mwari as God has them further confused. They will go to church because of fear of hell, and will accept Christ. They want to go to heaven. But, when it comes to needing help for now, they go to the N'anga and seek the help of the ancestors.

It's noteworthy that the biggest churches in Zimbabwe are Pentecostal. This is because they are offering power and deliverance. When a person is led to Christ in such a fellowship, the national leaders – knowing the cultural/traditional background from which all Zimbabweans come – insist on full deliverance immediately.

This frees the person from the bondage of ancestral and territorial spirit control. It also costs a lot, because they are cut off from their families and know full well that curses are being directed at them. But a person delivered in this way does not go back to ancestral worship.

Unfortunately, the missionary churches and the mainline denominations have not preached or taught these things. The Shona people know the power of the spirits, but do not see the power of God. The church is not proclaiming the truth about the reality of Satan and his demons.

Hence, the people sneak back and practice these spirit rituals secretly. They know there would be disapproval, but they do it anyway. The church has removed the miraculous quality from Christianity. The witch doctor has power, but Christ is presented as appearing to be a wimp – weaker than the spirit medium.

DAWN: What can the Church do to liberate people from this form of bondage?

CHIUNDIZA: It takes vision and courage to preach the liberating gospel. The mistake churches sometimes make is to attack the system and the structure of the territorial spirits.

This is a big mistake. It is very negative to go to a chief and tell him, 'You're a steward of demons.' That will not win him over. The church must preach a liberating gospel and be involved in the subsequent power encounter. The people need to see that through the power of Christ they can deal with these things in the spirit world.

My research is designed to help inform the church. My subject is 'Spiritual Warfare – The Only Way Forward.' Unless we have a breakthrough on this level, we're wasting our time.

The gospel must have greater power than the traditional system. Christ referred to the Spirit of God being upon him, anointing him to preach a liberating, powerful gospel to the poor. Christ didn't just give lectures. He preached with power.

The black leadership in the church is not theologizing enough. More and more of our own people – who have trained in the Bible schools and seminaries in the west – come back as extension cords of something that does not work here.

We need African leaders who know God, who can theologize and bring the Bible alive to our people, so that God is released from the pages of Scripture, so that he becomes real and delivers people.

The church won't grow or advance until it is freed from the captivity of these spiritual forces. We need a breakthrough in the spiritual realm. We've been praying, but missing the enemy. The intercession of Christians is not relevant until we know how to pray.

Our praying must be motivated by love. People who pray their bitterness and fears to God will not achieve anything. Like Christ, we must be prepared literally to die for the people we pray for. God said: 'I sought for a man to stand in the gap.'

If we're going to change this nation, we need intercessors who say 'Give me Zimbabwe or I die!' We will become properly aggressive to the enemy – because we love the people. It's dangerous to enter into intercessory prayer with the wrong spirit. We need a network of real intercessors, informed people, who will pray with humility before God. This is the only way forward.

14

Don't Underestimate the Opposition

by Paul B. Long

How did a Presbyterian missionary to the Congo (now Zaire) learn that evil spirits, indeed, occupy defined territories? In this fascinating anecdote Paul Long, who holds the Ph.D. degree from the Fuller Seminary School of World Mission in Pasadena, California, and who has served as a professor of missions at the Reformed Theological Seminary in Jackson, Mississippi, tells how his experience in ministering to the Baluba people forced him into a theological paradigm shift.

The Lord spoke to me with his strong hand upon me, warning me not to follow the way of this people .... When men tell you to consult mediums and spiritists, who whisper and mutter, should not a people inquire of their God? Why consult the dead on behalf of the living? To the law and to the testimony! If they do not speak according to this word, they have no light of dawn. Distressed and hungry, they will roam through the land; when they are famished, they will become enraged and, looking upward, twill curse their king and their God. Then they will look toward the earth and see

Excerpted from *The Man in the Leather Hat* by Paul B. Long, Grand Rapids, Michigan, Baker Book House © 1986 with permission.

129

only distress and darkness and fearful gloom, and they will be thrust into utter darkness (Isa. 8:11, 19–22).

Mungede had no son.

He had a happy Christian wife and two daughters, but no son.

He was director of the Boy's Home where some two hundred boys lived while they studied at the mission station, but he had no son.

He was the best hunter of wild guinea fowl in the Bibanga mission area and he was an elder in the local church, admired and trusted as a Christian leader. But Mungede was not happy, for he had no son.

Although he was one of my first and best friends among Africa's Baluba people, and although we worked, talked, hunted and prayed together, I did not realize how deeply Mungede was burdened and how heavy were the pressures from pagan relatives over his failure to father male offspring. Nor did I know, at that time, why a son was so necessary in tribal thinking. Therefore I was quite shocked when the pastor announced during morning prayers one day that Mungede had returned to his village and gone back to the old ways.

I just could not believe it. I thought I knew my friend. I thought we communicated on deep levels and shared openly with each other. But it was true – the tribal pressure for a son had forced him to leave his Christian wife who had given him only daughters, and to return to his village, taking on two younger women with the hope that they would bear him sons.

'Why are sons so necessary?' I asked the pastor.

'Daughters marry and go with their husbands to the village of his parents. Children all belong to the father – not the wife – in our customs. Only sons remain in the village, and only sons therefore can feed the ancestral spirits. If one does not show respect for his *Ba Nkambua* (dead ancestors), they will become angry and afflict the careless and ungrateful son. Furthermore, when a tribesman dies, he must leave a son to care for his spirit which remains in the village as an unseen member of the tribe.'

'Then Mungede is trusting tribal ways more than the teachings of the New Tribe, isn't he?'

'Yes,' the pastor replied, 'he has rejected the commandment of God which warns against communicating with spirits of the dead. He has gone back to the old tribe and is now caught in its darkness.'

I was determined to try and bring my friend back, so I traveled to his village, some five kilometers east of Bibanga station. When I found Mungede, I was shocked with the change in his appearance. His once radiant face was dark with the 'utter darkness' that marks the people under direct demonic direction. It was obvious that he had been talking with spirits and seeking their power in his life. But I had a problem. I did not believe that evil spirits could take over a life that had been transformed by faith in Christ. From a theological standpoint, it seemed impossible for the born-again believer to go back to his former slavery, but it looked like that was just what had taken place in Mungede.

We hunted guinea all day, rested in the shade, and talked at length about life, death and our hope for eternity. But Mungede was as closed as any pagan I had ever talked with; I could not reach him in any way.

After a good hunt, we returned to his house to rest while his wives prepared the guinea hens for our evening meal. Looking around the area, I was impressed with the fact that he had settled in the very center of spirit worship for the tribe. A medicine man sat nearby, along with three medicine women in the robes worn when communicating with spirits. The drums were there, as were the rattles, the charms, and the spirit mound. The mound looked like a good pulpit to me, so I asked Mungede to beat the drum and call the people to hear a word from God.

'You want to worship here?' he said. 'This is the devil's territory.'

'I can talk with God anyplace, Mungede, and any time I please. Don't you know that?'

'We will see,' he said as he pounded the talking drum. (I

never learned to 'talk' with the drum except to say, 'Kill the rooster, the preacher is here.' I left Congo before I was able to add, 'but leave the setting hen on her nest.')

A large crowd gathered around the spirit mound. I was surprised to see that the medicine man and women were amused – it's always nice to have people happy when you tell them God's Good News, especially when they are capable of being dangerous.

When I stood to speak, I felt the oppressive presence and power of overwhelming evil. The 'utter darkness' was suffocating me. I felt the cold fingers of death press around my throat and I could not speak. As I stood there in foolish helplessness, the medicine people laughed; it sounded like voices from hell.

I turned in utter defeat to sit down with Mungede. 'I can't speak here,' I said when my voice returned.

'You should have known better. This is the devil's turf. You have no right or power here.'

'Does God have any turf in this village?' I asked.

'Yes. On the other side of the village we used to have a Christian chapel. The building is gone, but the land still belongs to God.'

'If you will invite the people to go with us there, I will try again.' And when I passed the medicine man, I added, 'Come with us, powerful one, and hear about the "affair of God."'

'I will stay on my turf,' he answered. 'Here I have power.'

On the other side of the large village, I was led to a clearing where the outline of the former chapel was marked by a shallow ditch formed by rain washing over the grass roof. The rectangular outline was about ten feet wide and thirty feet long. I stood where I supposed a pulpit had been, invited the people to gather around, and noted with surprise that all those who had come with us – about seventy – were pushing to stand within the boundaries of the ditch. Apparently, they wanted to hear God's word while standing on God's turf.

In the seven years we had lived with the Baluba, I had never preached with such liberty in God's Spirit. The words flowed with power, clarity, and beauty well beyond my normal abilities in that language. The people who stood on God's turf were electrified with a strange power and their response was immediate and unanimous. 'We will rebuild God's house,' they announced, and by evening of the next day a new grass-roofed chapel stood on the site of the former building. A new house for a teacher was also constructed, and God's work was reborn in the village.

Mungede never returned to the New Tribe during my days in Congo, but continued to follow the ways of his people, looking for a son to feed his spirit after death. Instead of inquiring of God, he consulted with 'mediums and spiritists who whisper and mutter' – and demonstrate power enough on their own turf to shut my mouth. He consulted 'the dead on behalf of the living' instead of going to the Word of God. He looked to those who 'have no light of dawn,' the ones who 'will be thrust into utter darkness.'

Two things I learned well in that village called Nkumba: never to invade the devil's turf without clear orders from the Lord, and to move out of enemy territory when the battle is beyond me. It does not pay to underestimate the opposition.

15

SEVENTH TIME AROUND
Breaking Through a City's Invisible Barriers to the Gospel

by John Dawson

John Dawson of Youth With a Mission, who resides in Sunland, California, has written the most popular textbook on dealing with principalities and powers, Taking Our Cities for God *(Creation House). This much briefer piece condenses the teaching Dawson has been developing over the past few years, and is one of the most practical, how-to chapters in this book. Many others are now following his strategy for strategic-level spiritual warfare.*

Cordoba, Argentina is a city of proud and fashion-conscious people. Position, possessions, and appearance are of prime importance to 1.1 million living here, who are largely of German and Italian descent.

The Youth With a Mission team I led to Cordoba was made up of Christians from more than 20 nations. We were dressed simply, struggling with Spanish and carrying gospel literature. We really felt like nerds.

The crowds were there. Thousands of Argentines from all over the country had come to see the world soccer playoffs. But

From *Prayer Pacesetters Sourcebook*, edited by David Bryant, © 1989 Concerts of Prayer International, Box 36008, Minneapolis, MN 55435, used with permission of the author.

our witnessing seemed to lack power. No one was coming to know Christ. The next day, all 200 of us met for prayer in a rented monastery on the edge of town. We cried out to God for answer.

During that day of prayer and fasting, the Holy Spirit began to reveal the nature of the unseen realm over Cordoba. We realized that our timidity and weakness in proclaiming the gospel was partly due to satanic forces at work in the culture. We discerned a principality attempting to rule the city with 'pride of life.' The only way to overcome a spirit of pride is with the humility of Jesus. So, with the Holy Spirit guiding, we decided to come against the principality in the opposite spirit.

The next day our entire group went downtown. We formed smaller teams of about 30 and walked into the open-air malls. We knelt down right there in the midst of the fashion parade, surrounded by expensive bistros, sidewalk cafes, and boutiques. With our foreheads to the cobblestones, we prayed for a revelation of Jesus to come to the city.

Breakthrough was immediate – breakthrough in us and breakthrough in the city. Large crowds of curious people began to gather around each group.

I vividly remember how Christ strengthened me when I set aside my dignity and knelt in the street. The intimidation of the enemy was broken along with our own pride. As the crowd became larger, I stood to my feet and began to explain through an interpreter why we had come to the city. As I lifted my voice to communicate to the people at the edge of the crowd, the boldness and compassion of the Lord filled me.

All over downtown Cordoba that day, team members preached to attentive audiences. We reaped a harvest of souls. The people were receptive to the point of insisting that we autograph the gospel tracts we gave them! This warm response continued for several weeks until our departure.

Now tell me: how could a city so resistant to the gospel suddenly become a place of harvest? Satan holds the cities and nations by accusation and deception. These are his only weapons. When we minister in a city, we are hindered by that which is deceiving the people. In Cordoba, we were hindered by the spirit of pride that filled the city.

How do we overcome the enemy? We discern the nature of his deception and come in the opposite spirit. Being careful to resist temptation ourselves, we continue in united prayer until authority is gained and God breaks through.

Remember the story of Jericho? Militarily it made no sense to march around the city wall for seven days. But spiritually the Israelites were gaining authority through the exercise of faith, obedience and self-control. The fact that they had to march in silence is probably a clue to the nature of the unseen realm over Jericho. If they had responded to the insults and mockery hurled from the walls, a spirit of contention, pride, and anger might have been let loose among them. Instead, they walked in silent self-control until the victory shout, and by God's power the walls came tumbling down.

On a personal level, we go through this when a Jehovah's Witness or Mormon comes to our door. They are often empowered by a spirit of religion controversy. But the Bible says, 'We fight not against flesh and blood...' So our contest is with the deceiver – not the deceived (but sincere) person standing in front of us. In other words, if you get into an argument about the trinity and win, you lose. Far better to come in meekness as one who has a testimony of Jesus' mercy in your life.

What about spiritual oppression over nations? How do we approach the battle for South Africa, for instance? Apartheid is a spirit, not just a political phenomenon. It is a spirit that goes deep into African colonial history, with its roots in idolatry. When a good thing like cultural heritage is made into an idol, then injustice is the result. How do we shatter the power of the spirit behind apartheid? Through yielded rights and humble servanthood. We can rebuke the devil all day long and still be powerless unless we apply faith and obedience to a God-directed strategy.

A year ago I preached to a large, multi-racial gathering at the Durban Convention Center in South Africa. I spoke on the sin of unrighteous judgment and closed the message by leading us in repentance of racial stereotypes and prejudice. We each then washed the feet of someone of another race. Thousands of Afrikaners, Zulus, Indians, English and Colored wept in each other's arms as a spirit of reconciliation spread. This may seem like a small victory, but political reformation will grow only out of territory gained in the unseen realm. God's promise is: 'If my people, who are called by my name, will humble themselves and pray and seek my face and turn from their wicked ways, then will I hear from heaven and forgive their sin and will heal their land' (2 Chron. 7:14).

All over the world, praying Christians are agreeing about the nature of the battle for individual cities. For example, the prayer warriors of London believe they are battling a spirit of unrighteous trade that has influenced the world for hundreds of years through that great city. David exhorted the Israelites to 'pray for the peace of Jerusalem' (Ps. 122:6). I believe this was a strategic instruction, directing them against a spirit of religious controversy which had taken up residence in the holy city.

There was a time prior to the rise of today's nationalism when much of the world consisted of clusters of city-states like Venice or Luxembourg. Today, apart from Hong Kong, Singapore, still-surviving Luxembourg and a few others, the world consists of entities we call nations, which often have several world-class cities within their borders. In reality, a nation is a geo-political alliance among its cities. Cities are where the national myth is largely enshrined. The land between is relatively empty and serves only to sustain the life of the city. A nation is the sum of its cities.

As we dream of discipling nations, we need to understand their urban makeup. The gospel must transform the spiritual, philosophical, and physical life of a country's cities. If it does anything less, we have failed to win the battle.

The early days of the Salvation Army are a graphic example of the power of the gospel transforming the life of the city. General Booth and his followers clearly identified the satanic bondages prevailing at the time, including alcoholism and prostitution. They employed city-wide strategies which resulted in city-wide victories.

To effectively penetrate the city with the gospel, we must understand some truths of spiritual warfare.

1. Satan's kingdom is a limited hierarchy of evil spirits.

2. High ranking, supernatural personalities, referred to as principalities and powers in Ephesians 6, seek to dominate geographic areas such as the city, with all its peoples and subcultures.

3. We as believers are taught by God's Word to treat such beings with respect, but to 'take captivity captive' – to tear down the rule and authority of the evil one. Our authority is the result of Jesus' victory on the cross.

4. God's power is strategically applied by discernment of the unseen realm.

5. We must overcome the enemy before employing other methods of ministry among men and women.

In a given battle for a person, a family, a church or a city, discerning the nature of the enemy's lie is half the battle. Only after his deception is exposed can we exercise the authority of Scripture to thwart his schemes. Jesus resisted the devil this way during his time of temptation in the wilderness.

Whole countries are kept in darkness by satanic lies that have become cornerstones of a particular culture. For example, take the struggle with rejection and the fear of authority experienced by many Australians. Entering through the cruel roots of Australian history, Satan has been able to create a general distrust of all authority figures, including the highest of all – God himself. The truth is that Australia is not a nation founded on rejection and injustice, but a chosen people with as much dignity and potential as any people in history.

Isaiah 60 says that the people of the earth sit in gross darkness. Can you imagine walking into a darkened room filled with people who have spent their entire lives sitting there watching the TV images flickering in front of them, thinking that is all there is to reality? Imagine flipping the light switch on and asking everyone to examine the mundane equipment responsible for the illusion. Satan is a projectionist, an illusionist, a deceiver, the father of lies. The Bible says that one day we will look upon him in amazement saying, 'Is this the one that made the nations tremble?' (Isa. 14:16). He will be seen in reality as being small and impotent.

How can you contribute to victory in the battle for your city or nation? Begin by identifying the spiritual opposition and its unique manifestations.

1. Look at your city's secular history. Ask yourself the question, 'Why is this city here?' Is it just the project of geography and commerce or does God have a redemptive purpose in mind? Jonah was surprised at the way God looked at Ninevah. You, too, may be surprised when you discover what is oppressing people today. Psalm 115:16 says, 'The heavens belong to the Lord, but he has given the earth to all mankind.' In other words, this is our planet and the only authority that Satan has stolen is man's authority. He initially gains this authority when, at some point in history, human beings believe his lies and are seduced into allegiance to his plan. An obvious example would be the spirit of greed let loose during the California gold rush that still dominates much of San Francisco.

2. Look at your city's Christian history. Research the life of God's people in your city, particularly during times of revival. If you live in Los Angeles, a study of the Azusa Street revival would give you insight into today's battle. During times of revival, the supernatural realm is seen with great clarity, and often records are kept which contain important insights. Ours is a covenant-keeping God, and you may be amazed at the promises received by past generations – your spiritual forefathers engaged in the same battle. It is an important principle of humility to acknowledge and honor those who have gone before. It also inspires our faith. Because of God's covenant with David, Josiah's generation lived in a time of revival rather than judgment.

3. Identify your city's prophets, intercessors and spiritual elders. In every city there is what I call a hidden eldership – a group of saints that you will not find listed in any book. It consists of God's circle of mature believers who 'stand in the gap' until

victory comes. Isaiah 62:6 says, 'Upon your walls, O Jerusalem, I have set watchmen; all the day and all the night they shall never be silent. You who put the Lord in remembrance, take no rest and give Him no rest until He establishes Jerusalem and makes it a praise in all the earth.' Some of these 'watchmen' are obvious, such as veteran pastors. Others may be intercessors in obscurity or prophetic people with a premonition. If there is a common theme among those who are sensitive to the Spirit's guidance, you're on to something. God always confirms a strategy through several witnesses, and this is particularly important when dealing with demonic forces.

4. Study your city's demographics. It is amazing to me how ignorant we often are of the basic realities around us. Where do the people live? How many are in poverty? Why are they in poverty? Are there subcultures, ethnic groups, changes in the economy, an aging population – what's really going on?

Spiritual warfare doesn't operate in a vacuum. Jeremiah 29:7 says, 'Seek the welfare of the city where I have sent you into exile, and pray to the Lord on its behalf; for in its welfare you will have welfare.' This is an exhortation to Jews in Babylon who, like some modern believers, had a tendency to dream of a distant Jerusalem instead of recognizing the task at hand. Be grateful for your city. Study its potential, and you will receive the insight you need.

Once we know what we are up against, what should we do?

1. Begin with worship. Everything born of God goes through a very natural process. Worship is like an act of love that is followed by conception, gestation, travail, and birth. So always begin with worship. It is in the place of thanksgiving and praise that God conceives within us his mind and heart for our city.

2. Wait on the Lord for insight. Don't rely on finite reasoning or human cunning; what worked at Jericho didn't work at Ai. Learn to listen to God with child-like dependency, and he will guide you into victory. The Scriptures are full of exhortations about waiting on God. Psalm 40:1 says, 'I waited patiently for the Lord; he inclined unto me and heard my cry.' We are promised that God will speak if we seek him. 'My sheep hear my voice and they follow me' (John 10:27).

3. Identify with those you want to reach. When Nehemiah prayed for the restoration of Jerusalem, he didn't pray for the city as though he were not a part of it. He said, 'I and this people have sinned' (Neh. 1:6). Ezra went even further when he said, 'Oh my God, I am ashamed and embarrassed to lift up my face to thee, my God, for our iniquities have risen above our heads, and our guilt has grown even to the heavens' (Ezra 9:6). Both were righteous men. You, too, may be a righteous person who is not involved with your city's vices. But we can all identify with the roots of any given sin. Take, for example, the shedding of innocent blood in the act of abortion. You may never have participated in an abortion, but all of us have been guilty of the root sins – lust, the love of comfort, the love of money, rejection, unbelief. These common struggles can help us identify honestly with the sins of our city when we ask for God's mercy.

4. Minister in the opposite spirit. Is the enemy tempting you to be stingy or greedy? Come against it with exuberant generosity. Overcome pride with humility, lust with purity, fear with faith. Paul said, 'I can do all things through him who strengthens me' (Ph. 4:13).

5. Travail in prayer until God's purposes are birthed. That which is conceived by God eventually comes to birth. Just as the contractions of the uterus herald the beginning of labor, there are times when our souls are stirred by God's Spirit to seasons of intense prayer. Anyone who earnestly seeks God experiences such travail, but when the united Christians of a city are at this stage, it signals impending revival.

How do you perceive God? How big is He? The size of your God is revealed by your plans and expectations. His objectives are plain enough. Envision this, for example: God's heart for the city becomes your heart. You and your teammates begin a city-wide prayer movement. There is revival in the local churches, followed by an awakening among non-Christians, reformation of society, and new expressions of world mission.

Is your God big enough for that? He waits for people who will see him as he is and then follow him to victory.

142

Part III

THE ANALYSIS:

Perceptions and Perspectives

16

Territorial Spirits and Evangelization in Hostile Environments

by Vernon J. Sterk

Vernon J. Sterk is a field missionary of the Reformed Church of America, working among the Indians of Mexico. Some of the persecution of believers that he has witnessed seems to him to come from something other than simply human opposition to Christianity. In this chapter he raises the question as to whether some of this might be directly attributed to territorial spirits.

I want to address an often-forgotten factor in persecution and resistance to evangelization, the reality and work of demons and evil spirits, specifically 'territorial spirits.' Although this will not be simply a case study of the Tzotzil Tribes in Chiapas, Mexico, it will reflect on many of the events and illustrations which have come from my experience in that particular work. Because my awareness in the area of territorial spirits has only recently begun to surface, I will not be analyzing my own experience, but rather I will be compiling the available data and analyses in order to formulate a hypothetical framework upon which to base my own investigation. I will attempt to answer the basic questions: Are territorial spirits a reality? Should they be

Excerpted from an unpublished research paper written for the Fuller Seminary School of World Mission © 1989 with permission of the author.

considered as a factor in persecution? If territorial spirits find their main assignment in resistance to the gospel, how are we specifically to deal with them? These questions will set the theoretical framework for our analysis.

1. Satan and Spiritual Warfare

At the outset, it would be easy to simply make a generalized statement that all persecution and resistance to the gospel is the work of Satan. And even though it is not the central aim of this study, we must start there.

Satan is certainly behind all persecution and efforts to keep the message of Jesus Christ from penetrating the hearts of people and the core of cultures. We could even say that opposition to the gospel is probably his major role and goal. The words of 2 Cor. 4:4 refer clearly to the work of Satan when it says that 'the god of this age has blinded the minds of unbelievers, so that they cannot see the light of the gospel of the glory of Christ, who is the image of God.' And Scripture is clear about calling Satan 'the ruler of this world' (Jn. 12:31, 14:30, 16:11), 'the tempter' (Mt. 4:3), 'the evil one' (Mt. 13:38), and 'the one who deceived them' (Rev. 20:10).

Much has been written on Satan. There is general agreement about the reality of the power of Satan and the fact that we should never underestimate that power. Complete books line the shelves of the library which list Satan's titles and names (see Bubeck 1975), and offer good biblical studies on the origin, attributes, and work of Satan. Others have written on spiritual warfare and how we can best do battle with Satan (see Harper 1984). While these and others like them are valuable studies and are important for us to use in the spiritual battle that we experience all around us, many Christians in Latin America and others parts of the Third World are now telling us that such a concept of the personification of evil is not really adequate. They express their feelings that it is not only too vague and distant, but also does not fit what they see in reality and biblical revelation, to attribute all of the evil in the world to Satan.

Simply stated, many Christians are observing that the immediate work of evil and its destruction can be identified specifically as the work of 'territorial spirits.' That is to say that they actually experience the effects and presence of evil in a sphere that is much closer and more personal than the identity of Satan. In the battle against evil and in the challenge to preach the good news of Jesus Christ, they are finding it much more helpful to identify with the description of 'principalities and powers' (Eph. 6:12) than with a general more distant idea of 'Satan.'

In our first years of pioneer evangelism in the Zinacanteco tribe of the Tzotzil-speaking Indians in the Central Highlands of Chiapas, Mexico, my wife and I had many people come and explain that their illness was being caused by specific and identifiable evil spirits. Some would speak of a spirit that dwells in an underground stream of water running under their house. Others would see these spirits attacking them as they gathered firewood, or causing their children to fall and injure themselves. There were no Christians in that tribe, and we, as Western missionaries, were ill-prepared to approach these local manifestations of evil spirits. Our worldview caused us to find it easier to deny their existence and attribute all of this to a rather remote Satan. The Zinacanteco people were attempting to exercise some control over these evil spirits through shamans and a sacrificial system of curing ceremonies. They felt the need to handle specific and local spirit forces with specific and local ways of handling them.

As we noted earlier, one of the principal affairs with which Satan is preoccupied is to 'veil the gospel' (2 Cor. 4:3). But how does Satan do this? At this point in our discussion, I would like to introduce an idea to which I had given very little previous thought. C. Peter Wagner writes the following:

> It is helpful to remind ourselves that Satan does not possess the attributes of God, and therefore he is not omnipresent. Although he may be able to move from one place to another very rapidly, still he can be in only one

place at one time. Therefore, if he is intent on blinding the minds of the three billion who have yet to receive the light of the gospel of the glory of Christ, he must delegate this responsibility to others, namely evil spirits (Wagner 1990: 76).

In Matthew 12:24–28 Jesus spoke of the casting out of demons as an invasion of Satan's kingdom. Satan is described as 'the prince of demons' (v. 24). All of this would give us a fairly clear picture of Satan as the commander of an army of evil spirits who function as his agents in all parts of the world. Dick Bernal echoes what Peter Wagner has said:

> 'I call your attention to the fact that Satan is not omnipresent. He cannot be every place at one time. And so, he must dispatch chief rulers (principalities) to guard and protect his perverted scheme for empires, nations, provinces, states, and even cities' (Bernal 1988:23).

Satan delegates his power and authority to these evil spirits who quite probably number in the millions. One of the evil spirits that Jesus cast out (in Mark 5:9) gave his name as 'Legion, for we are many.' A Roman legion was made up of six thousand men, so we would certainly be able to say that in this one small area of Gerasa in that time there was a large number of territorial spirits actively working in Satan's hierarchy. And the great number of descriptions of evil spirits and demons in the Bible almost always denote them in the plural, as if they were associated with many others.

I am now convinced that Satan does work by delegation, and that there are many more demons and spirits in the world than we have ever realized. It may be that when there is a large representation of Christians in an area, the evil spirits are reduced in number or considerably weakened, but in an animistic Indian village where I lived and worked in southern Mexico that had no Christian presence, the ominous domination of that area was so oppressive that we could literally feel it, even though our worldview did not yet allow us to recognize the specific evil spirits that were identified by the Indian people. Even a non-Christian anthropologist who lived in that same village for six months commented to us about the spiritual oppression that she felt was so pervasive there. When a number of people from those villages became Christians, there was almost immediate and violent persecution. Was that persecution the direct responsibility of the territorial spirits that had been delegated power for that tribe or village? We only prayed general prayers for God to limit Satan's power in opposing the gospel, but we never took the local emissaries of the enemy into account, nor did we know how to handle them. Could that be why some of those areas are still extremely belligerent and resistant to the message of Jesus Christ, in spite of the use of the best missiological tools and approaches that could be mustered?

2. Territorial Spirits

All of the Tzotzil tribes, with whom we have worked for more than 20 years, can identify specific tribal deities which act as guardian spirits (saints and ancestral gods), and they can also name specific evil spirits that are in charge of the various kinds of evil in their culture. The *Yajval Balamil* or 'Earth Owner' controls sickness and curing through 'soul loss and redemption.' There are many demons, like the *Poslom* which takes the form of a ball of fire and attacks people at night to cause severe swelling. The *J'ic'aletic* or 'Blackmen' are looters and rapists who commit indiscriminate attacks of all kinds of evil. There is a seemingly endless list of frightening evil beings or spirits to which the Tzotzils refer to as *Pucujetic* 'devils' (Vogt 1969:304).

There is a very clearly defined specialization of the roles and evil work of the Tzotzil spirits, but of even more interest in this study, they also have territorial designations and assignments. This is true for both the evil spirits and for the Tzotzil 'guardian spirits.' The ancestral spirits reside in certain mountain peaks. Evil spirits can be contacted by a shaman in certain caves, and through specific cross shrines. All of the spirits have geographical limits for their power, even though the reach of the evil spirits seems to be more extensive than that of the guardian or ancestral spirits, whose assigned areas seem very limited. For example, Zinacanteco Indians have often expressed fear of going to lowland cornfields outside of tribal boundaries, because there they don't have the protection of guardian deities but the evil spirits 'travel around and find them.'

When Tzotzil Indians become Christians and undergo persecution, they often cite the power of territorial tribal evil spirits as the reason that they cannot continue to live in the tribal area. However, the pressure is a two-edged sword: they fear tribal spirits, but they also experience the threats of physical violence. Again, for the study of the role of territorial spirits in persecution and opposition to the gospel, it is very interesting to notice that the two factors seem to be intertwined. It appears that Tzotzil Christians attribute persecution more to the evil spirits involved than to the people who act it out against them.

Probably the most transparent example of the power of territorial spirits in the geographic boundaries of the Tzotzil tribes is seen when a sick person has a chance to go to the home of an evangelical Christian who is living outside of tribal boundaries because of persecution and expulsion. The person who is sick will usually choose to stay at a Christian home, outside of the territory of the tribal evil spirit, until he is completely well. If that person has carried an evil spirit with him or her in his or her body, the Christians pray in the name of Jesus to cast that spirit out and have it return from where it came.

In some cases, territorial spirits seem to be so fixed in a particular house or underground stream that everyone living in the immediate area is affected by sickness, mental illness, or serious attacks. Zinacanteco shamans encourage a family to leave that house or property rather than to even attempt dislodging the spirit from the area. Shamans officially declare the area *'cuxul'* (living) and there is great fear of inhabiting this occupied territory.

In other cases, the territorial spirits come as temporary invaders of homes. Shamans perform house ceremonies in which the Zinacanteco Indians believe that a demon takes the form of a 'hummingbird demon.' It is interesting to note that the shamans do not attempt to rid the area or house of the demon, but rather try to appease the territorial spirit with sacrifices so that it will cause no further suffering and fear.

On yet another level of territorial spirits, anthropologists have noted that there are particular ancestral spirits connected with the ceremonial circuits that surround the tribal center, certain sacred places, and the special crisis ceremonies that are carried out by shamans (Fabrega & Silver 1973:164–167). Because I have not, in the past, paid much attention to the concept of territorial spirits, I have not yet made an in-depth investigation of this phenomenon.

The Tzotzil tribes which I have just described in this case study are not the only area of the world where this territorial spirit phenomenon is taking place. Others such as James Marocco of Hawaii have observed what he calls 'cultural ethnic demons.' His study of this states: 'It is my contention that there is a definite demonic power that affects the particular geographical areas and population centers' (Marocco 1988:5). Nor is this a new thing that is just now beginning to surface. John Nevius, writing in the 1800s, describes a house in Ho-kia-chwang, China, where a wealthy family was brought to poverty by a local spirit (Nevius 1968:61–62).

Is the Concept of Territorial Spirits Biblical?
It is clear from empirical observation that a case can be made for the existence of territorial spirits and their role in persecution and resistance to the Gospel. However, is it biblical? Does the Bible indicate that we are up against territorial spirits in specific local settings, and not just facing a more generalized opposition from Satan?

Of course the passage that is most often cited is Ephesians

6:12, where there is an indication that we are up against 'principalities' and 'powers' and 'rulers' and 'spiritual hosts of wickedness.' But do these agents of Satan occupy or control specific areas or territories in our world?

Old Testament Examples

In the Old Testament there is much mention of the specific places such as 'places on the high mountains,' or specific hills or certain trees where the pagan nations had identified as locales for specific gods and spirits (Deut. 12:2). God gave specific instructions to the Israelites that when they possessed these places to live, they must destroy all semblances of these gods and cast out the names of these gods and spirits from those places. The different nations all possessed specific gods and evil spirits which had specific names such as 'Baal,' and 'Ashera' (Judges 3:7), and 'Ashtoreths' (1 Sam. 7:3–4). In 2 Kings 17:29 we read that 'each national group made its own gods in the several towns where they settled, and set them up in the shrines the people of Samaria had made at the high places.' Each national group had its own gods or principalities which had separate names and identities. 'The men from Babylon made Succoth Benoth, the men from Cuthah made Nergal, and the men from Hamath made Ashima; the Avvites made Nibhaz and Tartak, and the Sepharvites burned their children in the fire as sacrifices to Adrammelech and Anammelech, the gods of Sepharvaim' (2 Kings 17:30–31). These images that were made certainly represented already existing spirits and gods, and the Bible clearly defines them as evil (2 Kings 17:17). Deuteronomy 32:17 makes a clear connection of these foreign gods to 'demons.'

A very interesting observation on the power of territorial spirits is made in 1 Kings 20:23 where 'the officials of the king of Aram advised him, "Their gods are gods of the hills. That is why they were too strong for us. But if we fight them on the plains, surely we will be stronger than they."' This expresses a clear belief, at least among those people that spirits and gods had power only over certain limited areas of jurisdiction.

In the story of Naaman going to Elisha to be healed of leprosy, Naaman is told that he must go to wash in the Jordan where God would cleanse him, and not to the Damascus rivers of Abana and Pharpar which were in the domain of the god Rimnon (2 Kings 5:1–19). There are illustrations that indicate that many in Israel also saw God's territory as mainly the land of Canaan. When David was being pursued by king Saul, David expresses a fear of meeting death on some foreign soil, far away from the Lord. He says, 'Now do not let my blood fall to the ground far from the presence of the Lord.'

I believe that the above Old Testament references are helpful in understanding what the Ephesians 6:12 passage means when it speaks in the New Testament time of spiritual 'principalities and powers.' During the Roman occupation, most of the people of Israel also saw demonic personages located in specific political powers in specific places.

New Testament Examples

The examples of territorial spirits in the New Testament are limited. While there are many cases where demons and evil spirits are openly confronted, there are but a few times when the idea of those demons being attached to specific territories is recognized.

When Jesus was about to cast the demons from the possessed man (Mark 5:1–20), the demons begged Jesus not to send them out of that area. It would appear quite clearly that a legion of demons belonged to that area and did not want to leave. I also find it interesting to note that when the spirits were cast into the pigs and then into the lake, then the people of that region seemed to be blinded by the power of those demons for they were immediately afraid and began to plead for Jesus to leave their region (v. 17).

Although the connection is more difficult to demonstrate from the text, the story of Paul's extraordinary work in Ephesus (Acts 19) suggests that territorial spirits might have been at work. After Paul's open warfare with evil spirits (v. 12), we read the account of the seven Jewish exorcists who are overpowered and beaten by the evil spirit in a man. However, when power encounter in the name of Jesus brought many to openly believe, the goddess 'Artemis' stirred the mobs to oppose the gospel and start a riot. The principality named 'Artemis,' who appears to have been a principality over the evil spirits of that area, was likely in control of the area around Ephesus.

Although there are many other passages in the Bible which give confirmation of the hierarchy of Satan and many that indicate that there are numerous demons and evil spirits delegated by Satan, except for the ones cited above, there are few that give clear indications of them being territorial. However, I believe that the above examples do reveal that there are territorial spirits that do dominate certain areas, kingdoms, nations, and places. Even though I am sure, from the Biblical evidence, that Satan does not always use this territorial method or approach, I agree with C. Peter Wagner's hypothesis that:

> Satan delegates high ranking members of the hierarchy of evil spirits to control nations, regions, cities, tribes, people groups, neighborhoods, and other significant social networks of human beings throughout the world. Their major assignment is to prevent God from being glorified in their territory, which they do through directing the activity of lower ranking demons (1990:77).

The Major Assignment of Territorial Spirits: To Oppose Evangelization

The major task of preventing God from being glorified is carried out by the assignment of specific territorial spirits for the purpose of halting or disrupting evangelism in their territories. I am entirely convinced that the resistance which we experience in many areas of the world in the growth of the church is the direct result of demonic forces. I cannot say that they are always territorial spirits, but the more I hear of the experiences and work of those such as evangelist Omar Cabrera in Argentina, Christian psychologist Rita Cabezas in Costa Rica, and many others, the more clearly I begin to understand some of the things that we have seen in the work of evangelism among the Tzotzils in Chiapas.

Nabenchauc is a village in the high mountains of Chiapas where my wife and I lived for ten years among the Zinacanteco Indians. It is the largest of all of the Zinacanteco villages and boasts of hundreds of shamans. We experienced many world-view changing experiences of the reality and power of demons and evil spirits while we attempted to do pioneer evangelism there. When the power of the Gospel finally broke down a few of the walls in that village, the persecution became intense. God performed many healing miracles, and some power encounters have taken place. Yet, even after much general prayer pleading with God to break the power of Satan in that village, we have only seen small spurts of growth in which the new Christians are either forced to revert to animism or be harshly expelled from their land and homes. There has been more growth in other villages in that tribe, even though there has been much less evangelism done in some of those other villages, and God has concentrated less of his demonstration of power in those areas.

As I have read and studied about this phenomenon of territorial spirits, it all seems to fit. In the village of Nabenchauc, the shamans and tribal political bosses are also those who serve or control the 'cargo' positions which have direct contact with the local spirits and deities that are the 'owners' and 'demons.' They control all dimensions of life in the village, and any deviation from that control is met with various forms of persecution. Since the Gospel was first communicated in this village, there has been a great increase in the number of spirits and deities. This has been reflected in both the increased number of 'saint' images in the local church-shrine and in the amazing multiplication of house 'talking saints.' The resistance to the Gospel has corresponded with the increase in these spirits.

I wish that I could report that we have taken authority over these spirits in Jesus' name and the growth has become fantastic, but neither we who are missionaries nor the expelled

Zinacanteco Christians had ever considered this concept of specific territorial spirits. We never did more than pray general prayers against Satan's power in Nabenchauc, and the growth of the church has been generally slow and halting.

We have observed, on the other hand, that the greatest openness to the Gospel is shown when Tzotzils temporarily work, reside, or market outside of tribal boundaries. Many Tzotzils are open to the gospel and become believers when they go to work far away from the influence of their tribal areas.

Timothy M. Warner, professor of mission at Trinity Evangelical Divinity School, has stated: 'I have come to believe that Satan does indeed assign a demon or corp of demons to every geopolitical unit in the world, and that they are among the principalities and powers against whom we wrestle' (see page 52). As I recall accounts from all over the Tzotzil tribal areas where Christians have suffered serious resistance to the Gospel, I am becoming more and more convinced that anyone facing persecution should be aware that there are surely demons and evil spirits involved; and most likely they will be territorial spirits.

3. Dealing with the Territorial Spirits

Knowing that territorial spirits exist and that they may, in many cases of resistance to the Gospel, be the ones presenting the obstacles and causing the reaction of persecution, there remains another question: How do we deal with them?

It is possible that we should approach the battle with these territorial spirits the same way that is suggested by major authors for casting out any evil spirit or demon. Merrill Unger simply states that 'Demons are "dispossessed" in the Name of Christ' (Unger 1971:119). Michael Harper suggests that we have four basic weapons: '1) the Name of Jesus, 2) the Word of God, 3) righteousness, 4) the spiritual gifts' (Harper 1984:56–60). Harper also makes some important suggestions about practising the ministry of defeating the enemy. He is not speaking about demons at this point, but I believe that, for our present discussion, these weapons are valid in the battle against territorial spirits. He says that the first step is 'self-repentance and confession.' The second is 'deliverance' or the command to Satan and/or his agent spirits to get out. In prayer we bind Satan or an evil spirit. In this prayer we do not ask Jesus to do this; we do it in Jesus' name with the authority that Jesus has given us. Finally, we do not need to tell the spirits where to go, but we do need to follow up with a prayer for God to fill the area with the power of the Holy Spirit (Harper 1984:99).

I believe that one of the important roles that I must play as a missionary working with the Tzotzil Presbytery in Chiapas is to call the indigenous church leaders back to a ministry of 'aggressive prayer' in the battle against the principalities and powers. Many of them have come to assume that God has taken care of these evil spirits, and that they don't have to worry much about them. Thus, the 'command prayer' has almost fallen into disuse except in cases of obvious personal demon possession. Bubeck's reminder is timely: 'Aggressive prayer is a mighty, mighty part of the believer's effectiveness in spiritual warfare' (Bubeck 1975:113). Intercessory prayer is an important tool, but it is not how Jesus said that believers would drive out demons. Jesus makes it clear for 'those who believe: In my [Jesus'] name they will drive out demons' (Mark 16:17). Jesus Himself, in all of the Gospel accounts, commanded the spirits out. He did not pray to the Father to cast them out. And then He gave that power and authority to His disciples (Luke 9:1), and also to us. The Tzotzils must be called back to this ministry, especially in areas that have experienced severe opposition to the Gospel.

However, I have also come to see that in dealing with territorial spirits we may have some other factors to take into account. Before we assume that these spirits can be dealt with in the same manner as all others, we must investigate some specific areas about the battle with these very specific territorial spirits.

Identification of the Territorial Spirit by Name

One of the attempts that some of the writers in demonology make is to determine titles and names. In *The Adversary*, Mark Bubeck gives a detailed list of the names of Satan himself, giving 13 different titles (Bubeck 1975). However, neither he nor Michael Green (1981), nor Michael Harper (1984), make an issue of using the names of Satan or other demons to have more power in casting them out. Neither Unger (1971) nor Nevius (1968) take any special care about this issue, but then neither of them discusses the specific issue of territorial spirits. In Michael C.H. Koh's paper (Koh 1988:25), there is the recognition of the need for prayer and warfare on two levels: 1) the larger spiritual powers, and 2) the local or territorial power as in people movements and revivals. But he does not deal with the issue of names and identity.

Jesus only once asked the name of a demon (Mk. 5:9, Lk. 8:30) during His ministry, recorded in the New Testament. Daniel 10 does mention two names of territorial spirits. In Revelation 9:11 'the angel of the Abyss' is called in Hebrew 'Abaddon' and in Greek 'Apollyon.' The name 'Beelzebub' is used seven times in the New Testament, and appears to be a play on the words that were derived from 'Prince Baal.' The rest of the Biblical evidence would indicate that there is little emphasis on knowing the names of demons or territorial spirits.

On the other hand, there are several recent studies that indicate that these spirits are identifiable by specific names. Edward Langton, in *Essentials of Demonology* (Langton 1949), has done some analysis of the Persian names for demons which have meanings like 'Evil Mind,' 'Female Deceit,' and 'Wrath.' Manfred Lurker's *Dictionary of Gods and Goddesses, Devils and Demons* (1987) gives an extensive list of specific deity and demon names from all over the world of cultures throughout history. I have also discovered that the Apocryphal book of Tobit and Judith contains passages on 'Asmodeus' who is called 'the worst of demons' (Jerusalem Bible 524–532). Dick Bernal, in his book *Storming Hell's Brazen Gates*, says:

I cannot be too emphatic. In dealing with the princes and rulers of the heavenlies, they must be identified. Even the ancient Greeks knew how to approach their gods (whom we now identify as 'principalities'). They were always approached by name and title (Bernal 1988:57).

The Tzotzils, as I have indicated earlier, are very aware of the names of many of the territorial spirits that inhabit their tribal area and villages. They are even able to name some of those which occupy homes and streams. The shamans pride themselves in calling on the actual names of all of the different spirits and deities when they have very difficult cases. Therefore, for Tzotzil Christians to be able to name the spirits that they feel are opposing the Gospel in a particular area would probably be possible.

The question remains in all of this inquiry on names: Do we gain any special advantage in spiritual warfare by knowing the names of the spirits and demons? Many would agree with mark Bubeck's two bits of advice in dealing with evil spirits. He tells us not to believe them or their threats, and warns that we should not try to know too much about them (Bubeck 1975:124). However, if we do know the names of specific territorial spirits, there may be some validity in addressing the spirit by name when attempting to take over an area in Jesus' name.

It may be valid that we are able to use the names of specific territorial spirits in cases of persecution and sever opposition and hostility to the Gospel. Yet, I am very suspicious of names that are given by territorial spirits themselves, since I do not believe that they are about to reveal any secrets which would lead to their own downfall. Jesus Himself knew that: 'Any kingdom divided against itself will be ruined, and a house divided against itself will fall. If Satan is divided against himself, how can his kingdom stand?' (Luke 10:17–18a). However, this does not invalidate the using of specific names in casting out these spirits.

In many cultures there is the recognition that to give someone your name gives them a certain power over you. The

Tzotzil people have strong feelings about knowing the name of their 'animal spirit companion' (Vogt 1969:371). If some enemy gains knowledge of the name of that spirit, he can place a curse on that person by harming that particular animal spirit.

The Bible pays careful attention to the power that is embodied in names, especially in the 'Name of God' and in the 'Name of Jesus.' Deuteronomy 12:11 is an example of how the tabernacle was referred to as 'a dwelling for his Name.' In Solomon's message about the building of the temple he describes his plan 'to build a temple for the Name of the Lord...' (1 Kings 5:5). Many of the studies that have been done on the concept of 'name' in the Old Testament indicate that in the Hebrew culture the name itself signified something important about the character and personality of a specific individual. The name seems also to have revealed a similar identity in reference to God or other deities.

The New Testament gives even clearer indication that there is power in a name. Jesus said: 'And I will do whatever you ask in my name...' (John 14:13). To use the name of a person implies a certain authority granted by that person. In James 5:14 we are told to heal the sick 'in the name of the Lord,' and in Mark 16:17 Jesus says 'In my name they will drive out demons.' Again in Luke 10:17 the seventy-two that Jesus sent out came back to report: 'Lord, even the demons submit to us in your name.' In John 17:11 Jesus prays to the Father for his disciples: 'Holy Father, protect them by the power of your name – the name you gave me...'

All of this may not give any conclusive evidence of how we might use the actual names of specific territorial spirits or demons when we are dealing with them. However, some hypothetical conclusions may be helpful. First, we should not place much credibility in names given to us by a territorial spirit. It may be pure deception. Second, we may use the name of a specific spirit if it has been revealed or confirmed by a source other than a demonic one. Third, I do not think that we risk too much in using the names that are common knowledge to the people of an area or village, when these spirits have been known for generations to exert control over specific areas or territories. Fourth, we should use the general or functional names of demons or spirits if the actual names are unknown to us.

Finally, in this discussion on the importance of knowing the names of territorial spirits, we must not neglect the gift of discernment. One of the specific spiritual gifts available to the Church of Jesus Christ in spiritual warfare against territorial spirits is the discerning of spirits. I Corinthians 12:10 counts 'the discerning of spirits' as a gift given to us for 'mutual profit.' Certainly, this spiritual gift would be of great value not only in any ministry of deliverance, but it is essential in dealing with territorial spirits, especially in discerning of their specific names.

Conclusions

While we began this study with the assumption that Satan is the overall head of the hierarchy of evil in this world and is certainly behind all persecution and resistance to the gospel, we have seen clearly that he is not alone in his spiritual warfare against the kingdom of God. Around the world, Christians are experiencing the threats and the actual presence of evil forces that are specific and geographically located. It is, therefore, an oversimplification and underestimation of the enemy to simply reflect the obvious fact that Satan is the force behind all of the opposition to the gospel. We must take an honest look at the reality of territorial spirits.

The Tzotzil worldview is full of many local spirit-owners which are specific and geographical, much like those described by Loewen (see Chapter 17). It would seem that these territorial spirits have been delegated authority by Satan to oppose the Gospel in a specific area. Thus, the territorial spirits are the main agents in building resistance to the gospel of Jesus Christ in places like the Tzotzil tribes. A careful analysis of the territorial spirit concept reveals that they not only exist but that they are also responsible for the severe persecution and expulsion of Christians.

In tracing the Biblical examples of territorial spirits, we find in both the Old Testament and the New Testament that Satan has used territorial spirts to control nations, regions, tribes, and other smaller places. The main assignment of territorial spirits is the halting of evangelism. This is reflected in the Zinacanteco example.

To deal with territorial spirits, we must use aggressive command prayer. We address these spirits with their actual names if and when they are known, but we should not place too much emphasis on a proper name identity. It is important to identify the territorial spirit by a traditional name or a functional name. In all of the problem of identification, the gift of discernment of spirits is essential.

Finally, there are some serious dangers. We must heed a word of caution so that we do not lose a correct balance, and so that we do not get involved in a use of power that is not a part of God's will for us and the church. I certainly do not want to suggest an involvement with principalities that will ultimately do great damage to individuals and to the church in Chiapas. However, there is also the great risk of doing nothing because of our questions and fears. That would, in effect, negate the validity of this entire study, and it would allow the territorial spirits to continue to cause resistance to the gospel and persecution of Christians around the world.

I conclude from this study that a balanced ministry in the area of territorial spirits could be God's method of opening new doors for effective evangelism of which not only I, but many Christian leaders around the world, have not been aware.

References Cited

Bernal, Dick. 1988. *Storming Hell's Brazen Gates*. San Jose, CA: Jubilee Christian Center.

Bubeck, Mark I. 1975. *The Adversary: The Christian Versus Demon Activity*. Chicago: Moody.

Fabrega, Horacio Jr. and Daniel B. Silver. 1973. *Illness and Shamanistic Curing in Zinacantan*. Stanford: Stanford University Press.

Green, Michael B. 1981. *I Believe in Satan's Downfall*. Grand Rapids: Eerdmans.

Harper, Michael. 1984. *Spiritual Warfare: Recognizing and Overcoming Evil Spirits*. Ann Arbor: Servant Books.

Koh, Michael C.H. 1988. 'Intercessory Prayer and the Kingdom of God.' (An unpublished paper for Fuller Seminary School of World Mission)

Langton, Edward. 1949. *Essentials of Demonology*. London: Epworth.

Lurker, Manfred. 1984. *Dictionary of Gods and Goddesses, Devils and Demons*. London: Routledge & Kegan Paul.

Morocco, James. 1988. 'Territorial Spirits' (Unpublished thesis in Wagner office file.)

Nevius, John L. 1968. *Demon Possession*. Grand Rapids: Kregel Publications.

Unger, Merrill. 1971. *Demons in the World Today*. Wheaton: Tyndale House.

Vogt, Evon Z. 1969. *Zinacantan: A Maya Community in the Highlands of Chiapas*. Cambridge: Belknap.

Wagner, C. Peter. 1990. 'Territorial Spirits,' *Wrestling with Dark Angels*, C. Peter Wagner and F. Douglas Pennoyer, eds., Ventura: Regal Books.

17

Which God Do Missionaries Preach?

by Jacob Loewen

Jacob Loewen is an outstanding Christian anthropologist who served as a Mennonite Brethren missionary to Colombia, then for several decades as a translation consultant with the United Bible Societies in South America and Africa. In the extended version of this article which first appeared in Missiology: An International Review, Loewen makes a case that many missionaries fall into the danger of communicating to tribal peoples a concept of God which may appear to the people to be more like the territorial and functional 'gods' whom they serve rather than the universal, supreme God the missionaries are intending to communicate.

In setting the context for his argument, Loewen presents information about the territoriality of pagan demonic spirits which readers of this book will find very helpful. He also mentions some biblical passages in the Old Testament where not only did the Gentile pagan groups assume spiritual territoriality, but also where the Hebrews themselves were wrestling with concepts which could tend to suggest limitations to God's omnipresence and omnipotence. It is little wonder that some of us could be in danger of falling into similar traps today.

Excerpted from *Missiology: An International Review*, Vol. XIV, No. 1, January 1986, © American Society of Missiology, with permission.

For our purposes here, only Loewen's background material is reproduced. It is the part most apropos to understanding territorial spirits.

* * * * *

A new missionary to Nigeria was deeply thrilled when he got a land grant from the local king so that he could begin to build a mission hospital. Once the building began, he started each workday with Bible study and prayer for his work crew. Long before the hospital was ready to function, all his workmen had 'accepted Christ,' and the missionary felt that even the construction time had been an evangelistic success.

Once the building was completed all the workmen returned to their respective home villages, and the missionary began organizing a series of evangelistic tours through some of those same villages. To his complete chagrin he found that his 'converts' were contentedly tending idol shrines in their home villages. When he confronted them with what to him was a gross incongruity with their confession of faith as Christians, they in turn expressed their surprise at his abysmal ignorance; surely he knew that at the mission they had prayed to *owo* (God) because they saw that he was the one who had power there, but he was not in charge here in their home villages. Here they had to pray to the 'deity that owned this area.' 'If we try to pray to your mission God here, the local deity would be very, very unhappy and make too much trouble for everybody,' they affirmed with conviction.[1]

This African experience highlights the important truth that many, if not most, tribal and peasant societies experience their deities as tribally, geographically, or functionally specialized.

Western people who believe in God, especially Western missionaries who go overseas, feel very comfortable that they represent a God who is universal and who possesses the whole gamut of all-attributes. He is omnipotent, omnipresent, omniscient, and so on. Furthermore, Western Christians read the Bible and see only this all-embracing God. Their own worldview has blinded them to the fact that the Bible records the tremendous struggle which God waged with the Hebrew people, first of all, truly to become the only God of that tribe, and then to have them catch at least a few glimpses of the fact that he was really also the God of all mankind.

Deity as Territorially Linked

When my wife and I began our mission work in Colombia, one of the first things that struck us was that the Indians there saw every tree, mountain, stream, spring, or even large rock as being the home of some specific spirit entity. When I began to travel more widely during a dialect survey of Choco languages, I discovered that it was next to impossible to take people from one river or dialect to visit another dialect group because the people were afraid that the spirit powers of that new area, to which they were alien, would steal their souls and thus cause their death.[2] In group after group there are stories about hunters who in the pursuit of game had inadvertently gone beyond the domains of friendly spirits into the domains of alien spirits and of the dire consequences that had followed. Only a few had returned to tell the tale, and even some of those who did make it back died soon thereafter because they were unable to retrieve their souls from the alien spirits that had captured them.

Already some readers will feel that I am not talking about *God* but that I am talking about *spirits*. And in a way that is true, but it also points to a second important reality: most tribal and peasant peoples experience deity at least at two (and some at many more) levels. The first is at the so-called 'high-God' level, and the second is at the level of 'gods, spirits, fetishes, or ancestors,' and so on. (Each of these may form several separate levels of deity.)

The *high-God* concept has been eloquently expounded by the early Catholic missionary-anthropologist Wilhelm Schmidt (1965:21–33). This high God is the creator of the universe and usually also of men, but frequently a more personal or more

tribaly related deity plays the second role. After creation, however, something akin to the fall-of-man story recorded in
Genesis 3 occurred and the high God withdrew leaving men in
charge of, or under the domination of, lesser gods, spirits, or
even shades of their ancestors.

The accounts of this rupture between God and mankind are
as varied as the peoples who tell them. For the Waunana of
Colombia, where we began our missionary experience, it was
precipitated by direct intervention of *dosiata*, 'the devil,' who
caused the people to mistrust God and to buy axes from the
trickster-devil to be able to raise food crops independent of
their God. This act of mistrust caused *Ewandama*, 'the tribal
high God,' to withdraw from the *Waunan*, 'the people,' and left
them to fend for themselves against *dosiata's* kith and kin and a
host of other amoral spirit entities that inhabited their environ-
ment (Loewen 1969:156–157).

West Africans often speak about creation time as the time
when the high God/sky God had placed his abode (heaven)
very close to earth. At that time the people, really the women
(shades of Eden) who did the gardening, used long-handled
hoes and they continually poked into the sky or God's 'but-
tocks,' as one of the local languages puts it. God told the
women to use short-handled hoes, but they wouldn't. Finally
he got so tired of having his bottom poked that he withdrew
from the human scene leaving the people 'in the care of' their
deceased ancestors. Subsequently everyone began using the
current short-handled hoes (about 20 to 24 inches long), but in
spite of this God has kept himself and his abode at a distance
from humans on earth ever since. In another situation it was
the smoke from the woman's cooking fire that got into God's
eyes and caused him to withdraw in a huff (Cardinall 1970:15).

The parallelisms between these many different myths and
the biblical accounts are striking. In Genesis 1 it is the high
God/*El Elohim* who creates the universe. The setting of the
rupture is a garden/gardening scene. The immediate vehicle
for the rupture in the Bible, as in many African accounts, is the
woman. The cause is human unbelief or disobedience to God's

command, and the universal result is the current distance between God and mankind, usually spoken of as God's withdrawal, or in the Bible as man's ejection from the garden and presence of God.

As already said earlier, often the high God and the tribal God are one and the same, but not always so. In some cases we have the high God creating the universe and the tribal god creating the people and their culture. We see something very similar in the Bible where we actually find two creation accounts: one by *Elohim*, 'the high God' (Gen. 1–2:4a) and the other by *Yahweh*, 'the tribal God of the Hebrews' (Gen. 2:4aff.).

The Owners

In many societies throughout Central and South America the spirit deities associated with various geographical or topographical phenomena are spoken of as their 'owners.' Thus nomadic Indians in the Paraguayan and Argentina Chaco always 'consulted' the spirit owner of an area before they made camp. If the response was favorable they made camp in peace; if it was unfavorable, they would move to another area and repeat the process. Spirit forces 'owned' the land and, in the case of sedentary people, the land, in turn, is said 'to own' the people living on it. People never own the land; they only use it by the permission of its true spirit owners who, in a sense, 'adopt' them.

For many tribal groups, like those of Australia, the area controlled by friendly spirits, or owners of the land who have adopted them, is coterminous with land over which a tribe is willing to roam. For this reason war against another tribe for the purpose of taking away land is really inconceivable to them. It would be suicidal for a people to try to occupy land whose owners had already adopted another tribe, or which was watched over and lived in by the souls of the deceased ancestors of a people other than their own. For such people conquering another tribe's land invariably means that one must change religion; one must worship the local deities. For example, when the Zulus and their related tribes of South Africa conquered tribes as far north as today's Malawi and Tanzania, they immediately accepted the local gods. Thus in modern Malawi among the Ngoni (as the conquerors are called today) it is almost impossible to find even a trace of their earlier South African deities.[3]

The practical result of deities restricted to specific tribes or defined areas is that morality also is often similarly restricted. Proscriptions on negative behavior apply only to one's in-group. Thus to steal from, to harm, or to kill a person from one's own group is punished, but if one does these things to a member of another group one becomes a hero. This type of morality limitation is one of the major obstacles the newer nations of the third world have to overcome in their efforts to build a national identity. On the international scene, we see it especially in times of war when ordinarily law-abiding people become heroes when they kill, rape, and loot the enemy. Internally,Western nations experience it in various kinds of interracial or intergroup conflict as a result of which some groups feel free to bomb, burn and loot members of an out-group.

The Specialization of Deity

So far we have been speaking about deities identified with certain ecological or topological features, but deities can also be specialized functionally as to their activities. Most Westerners have at least some acquaintance with the Greek or Roman mythology and so have some awareness of special gods associated with or responsible for certain activities. Note the following condensed list of Greek and Roman deities and their areas of specialization.

Function	Roman	Greek
king of the gods	Jupiter	Zeus
god of the sun and youth	Apollo	Apollo
god of war	Mars	Ares

god of the sea	Neptune	Poseidon
messenger of the gods	Mercury	Hermes
god of wine	Bacchus	Dionysus
goddess of agriculture	Ceres	Demeter
goddess of hunting	Diana	Artemis
goddess of love	Venus	Aphrodite
goddess of the home	Vesta	Hestia

In South American tribes the specialization is largely among evil spirits; for example, the Lengua of Paraguay identify several dozen kinds of evil spirits, each of them with its own specialized function (Loewen 1965:280–306).

In Africa, on the other hand, especially among many Bantu tribes where the spirits are usually former human souls, the specialization is often most marked among the protective spirits. Thus it is not at all uncommon in West Africa to find a hierarchy of specialized spirits or deities.

Tribal people, however, are not the only ones who engage in such syncretism. We can see the Greco-Roman tradition of specialized deities has been carried on in many Catholic churches in the form of the saints which range from Saint Joseph, the patron of carpenters, to Mary Magdalene as protectress of the prostitutes. In Latin-America Christopaganism many local specialized deities have been saved from oblivion by being rebaptized with the name of a Catholic saint (Madsen 1957; Herskovitz 1937).

The Bible and Divine Territoriality and Specialization

In regard to the presence of deity in topographical phenomena, the Old Testament frequently speaks of the high places on which the people offered sacrifices to the God who was seen as residing there (1 Sam. 9:12–13; 10:5; 1 Kings 3:2; Hos. 2:13, etc.). Usually, however, *high places* were associated with Baal ('high places of Baal' in Numbers 22:41),or other alien deities (Levi. 26:30; 1 Kings 11:7–8; 17:9–10, etc.). Sometimes these mounds had been artificially built (1 Kings 15:23–24; 2 Kings

17:9); other times they were natural elevations like hills or mountains (2 Kings 17:10–11; Ps. 121:1; 2 Chron. 21:11).

That certain gods were rulers of certain territories and could only be worshipped there is also evident in a good number of biblical passages. It stands out very boldly in the case of Naaman, the Syrian general who was leprous. He disdainfully claimed that the waters of the Syrian rivers of Abana and Pharpar were as efficacious as those of the Jordan River, but when he was healed by bathing in Jordan's waters, he realized the power of the Yahweh of Israel and said: 'I know that there is no God in all the earth but in Israel.' But since he had to serve his king in Damascus, he asked the prophet for 'two mule burdens of Israelite earth' so that he could pray and worship Yahweh on Yahweh's own soil because his birth and his position condemned him to live in the domain in which the god Rimmon was the controller (2 Kings 5:1–19).

The Hebrews themselves accepted the territoriality of God. When Jacob, after his dream at Bethel, takes leave of Yahweh, the God of his fathers, and of his territory in order to go to Haran where *El* was enthroned, he says: 'If Elohim (the high God) will go with me and keep me in the way that I go ... so that I may come again to my father's house in peace, then Yahweh will be my Elohim' (Gen. 28:18–22).

And again, when Jacob is to return to Canaan, we read that Yahweh appears to him in a dream and says, 'I am the God of Bethel, where you anointed a pillar and made a vow to me. Now arise and go forth from this land and return to the land of your birth.' Here God (Yahweh) himself is presented as identifying himself with a specific place and with a specific land.

In Hosea we find some very poignant references to this problem. The prophet, or God by the mouth of the prophet, reminds them that they, the Israelite people, had made a covenant with Yahweh in the desert (Hos. 2:15; 9:10; 11:1; 13:4–5), but that when they entered the land of Canaan and their lifestyle changed from pastoral nomads to sedentary agriculturists, then they, the people of Israel, seemed to be afraid to trust Yahweh for fertility in the new land, and again and again turned to worship the Baals, who were the local agricultural-fertility deities. Thus Yahweh complains that Israel didn't recognize that it was he who gave them rich produce and that they attributed their prosperity to Baal's blessings (Hos. 2:8). In fact, Yahweh wonders aloud whether it would help if he would take them back to the desert (Hos. 2:14), where he first made the covenant with them.

This situation described in Hosea is very similar to the situation which we described for Africa where the conquerors felt obliged to accept the gods of the conquered because the latter's deities controlled the land. Thus Yahweh complains: As soon as they entered the land at Adam (Hos. 6:7, GNB) they broke their covenant with me and began to follow after the Baals. And even once they had been well established in Canaan 'the more Yahweh blessed their fields, the more they pursued the local Baals' (Hos. 10:1–2). In fact, the more Yahweh pressed them to be faithful to him, the more they worshipped idols (Hos. 11:1–2). Israel seemingly did not have the faith that Yahweh, the God of manna, quail, and water of the Negev, could really provide agricultural fertility in Palestine.

A most striking example of people having to accept the local gods in order to prosper is recorded for us in 2 Kings 17. After the Assyrians had carried off the Israelite population, they decided to fill the vacuum they had created there by transplanting large groups of people from other conquered areas. The groups that were transplanted into Israelite territory are listed together with their gods (17:30) as follows:

People	God
Babylonians	Succoth Benoth
Cuth	Nergal
Hamath	Ashima
Ivvah	Nabhaz and Tartak
Sepharvaim	Adrammelech and Anammelech

These new settlers did not worship Yahweh (Lord), and so the lions began to raise so much havoc among them that the governor sent a complaint to the Assyrian emperor that the immigrant transplants did not 'know the god of the land and so the god had sent lions, which were killing them' (2 Kings 17:25, GNB). The emperor at once recognized the problem – these people were not worshipping the god who controlled the region, and so, to remedy that situation, he sent the Jewish priests back to Samaria from Assyria 'to teach the people the law of the god of that land' (2 Kings 17:25, GNB).

Another biblical example of the belief in the territorial or ecological specialization of the gods is found in 1 Kings 20:23ff. The Syrians, under Benhadad, had suffered a severe defeat at the hands of the Israelites (1 Kings 20:19–20), but within a year they rebuilt their armies and planned a new campaign, and this time they took the deity factor into account. They reasoned: 'The gods of Israel are mountain gods, and that is why Israel has defeated us. But we will certainly defeat them if we fight them in the plains' (1 Kings 20:23, GNB).

Endnotes

1. A personal communication from Dr. Eugene Bunkowske.
2. In fact, when I did bribe (with the promise of a large cast-iron pot) the wife of one Indian to encourage her husband to accompany me to our home on the other side of the mountain range, I soon found myself battling with a dying man – his soul had been apprehended by the locals, and unless he got back quickly and had home spirits recuperate his soul, he was a dead man. Only by my praying aloud beside him for a whole night could I arrest the death process. Every time I fell asleep he resumed dying.
3. It has been noted by Nida, McGavran, and others that immigrant populations are usually most likely to change religion. It is possible that this observed fact is related to the regional deity – moving into another area requires a new God and a new religion.

References Cited

Cardinall, A.W. 1970. *Tales Told in Togoland*. Westport: Negro Universities Press.
Herskovitz, M.J. 1937. 'African Gods and Catholic Saints in New World Religious Belief,' *American Anthropologist*, 39:635–643.
Loewen, Jacob A. 1965. 'Mennonites, Chaco Indians and the Lengua Spirit World,' *Mennonite Quarterly Review*, October, pp. 280–306.

Loewen, Jacob A. 1969. 'I. Myth and Mission: Should a Missionary Study Tribal Myths?' *Practical Anthropology*, 16:147–185.

Madsen, William. 1957. *Christo-Paganism: A Study of Mexican Religious Syncretism*, New Orleans: Middle American Research Institute.

Schmidt, Wilhelm. 1965. 'The Nature, Attributes and Worship of the Primitive High God,' in W.A. Lessa and E.Z. Vogt (eds.), *Reader in Comparative Religion*, pp. 21–33.

18

Principalities and Powers

by Michael Green

Michael Green is both a scholar and a practitioner. As will be seen in this chapter, he does a thorough job of drawing on historical, biblical and theological material to provide us a picture of just what we are dealing with in strategic-level spiritual warfare. Although it is not explicit here, Michael Green's basic reason for grappling with these issues of spiritual warfare does not arise from overfascination with the devil and his forces, but with a burning passion to see men and women be transformed by the power of God from the kingdom of darkness to the kingdom of light.

As professor of evangelism at Regent College in Vancouver, British Columbia, Green not only teaches theories of evangelism, but he leads his students out in evangelistic missions where the true spiritual battles really are.

* * * * *

There is, in the heart of Oslo, a park where a fascinating display of bronzes adorns a large bridge and monument beyond it. The artist, Gustav Vigeland, is expressing his philosophy of

Excerpted from *I Believe in Satan's Downfall* by Michael Green, Grand Rapids, Michigan, William B. Eerdmans Publishing Company © 1981 with permission.

life, and nowhere is it more clearly portrayed than in the central figures on either side of the bridge. One is of a man, one of a couple; and they are both gripped, encased by a circle from which they cannot break free.

Modern man feels that bondage. So did ancient man. Perhaps nobody has been grasped the flavour of Graeco-Roman paganism than Edwyn Bevan. He wrote in *Hellenism and Christianity*:

> When men looked up at the stars, they shuddered to see there powers whose mysterious influence held them in a mechanism of iron necessity; they were the World-Rulers who fixed men's destiny without any regard to human will and human tears. Effort, shrewdness, long-laid design could bring no liberation from the predestined law... It became an obsession. This earth, the sphere of their tyranny, took on a sinister and dreadful aspect.

Judaism shared this sense of bondage to forces beyond themselves. They were not so materialistic as to locate them in the stars, but rather in the principalities and powers which were at work in the universe. The matter is sufficiently important for us to examine it in some detail.

The Principalities and Powers in Jewish Belief

When seen against the background of the demon-ridden world of the Middle East, Judaism presents a very different emphasis, concentrating on the one God, Creator of heaven and earth. However, the Old Testament teaches that there are many subordinate spirits under God's overall sovereignty.

Sometimes in the Old Testament we read of the *kedoshim*, or 'holy ones,' a heavenly court presided over by the Lord himself (Ps. 89:6, 8; Job 15:15; Deut. 33:2; Zech. 14:5). Frequently God is called *Yahweh Sabaoth*, 'Lord of the powers,' and here the gods of polytheism are seen as captives under his suzerainty. As we read of the *bene elohim* or 'sons of God' in

178

Job, the Psalms, and Genesis 6:3. But perhaps the most important passage of all is Deut. 32:8 where the best texts read that the God 'fixed the bounds of all the peoples according to the number of the *bene elohim*, the sons of God. For the Lord's portion is his people, Jacob his allotted heritage.' The meaning is well brought out elsewhere: Deut. 4:19 speaks of the moon, stars and hosts of heaven which the Lord has allotted to all the peoples under heaven, with the exception of Israel whom he has appointed for himself. Thus 'He appointed a ruler for every nation, but Israel is the Lord's own portion' (Eccles. 17:7).

In this way the Jews resolved the problem of the one and the many. There was only one God, and he was their God for ever. All other spiritual forces, be they good or bad, were ultimately of his creation, under his control and assigned as tutelary deities to other nations. Thus in the apocalyptic book of Daniel we find Michael appearing as God's champion for suffering Israel against the angel-prince (*sar*) of Persia and of Greece (Dan. 10:13, 20f, 12:1f). The nations which ruled the ancient world were under the supervision of their angel-princes, who in their turn were under the ultimate control of Yahweh, the Lord of heaven and earth, who had entered into a covenant relationship with his people Israel.

The Principalities and Powers in the Graeco-Roman World

As in any polytheistic culture, spirit forces figured largely in the Graeco-Roman culture into which Christianity was born. The world was subject to the guardianship of spirits, *daimones*, and the whole point of magic was to use formulae or objects to influence these 'world rulers' or 'elemental spirits.' The physical objects and the spiritual powers associated with them were often given no clear distinction. Thus the Greeks used 'Hephaestos' to mean both fire and the deity which supervised fire.

Another branch of this interpretation of the human and the

superhuman was given emphasis in the concept of *daimones*. These were spiritual deputies of the gods (or God) who ruled the world. They had many names, 'principalities, powers, rulers, thrones, world rulers, elemental spirits' and the like. It was from their clutches that men sought salvation through means ranging from philosophy to the occult. In a long line of writers, embracing Porphyry, the Mermetica and Celsus, these *daimones* (which act as intermediaries in the divine government of the world and as forces behind the human rulers and their state) are seen to be both bad and good. The good ones do not harm man, but preside over the state, commerce, medicine and the rest. The bad ones are not officially appointed by the gods but make up for this by trying to usurp authority, attract worship to themselves and denigrate the great gods (*Corpus Hermeticum* 16:13f, Origen, *Contra Celsum* 5:25, 7:68). The Christian writer Origen is not keen to establish any common ground with his pagan opponent, so he calls the evil spirits *daimones* and the good ones angels; none the less, he is operating with precisely the same cosmology. It was very widely accepted in antiquity that behind the rulers of the state, lay their *daimones* – or, as some preferred to call it, the *numen* or *genius* of the ruler. There is, in short, such a correspondence between the world of sense and time and the invisible world that the two were, to the ancients, almost a single entity. As Philo put it, the one God rules through his powers or angels (*Conf.* 171, 181 and *Leg. Alleg.* 3:177f).

The Principalities and Powers in the New Testament

Their prevalence
Oscar Cullmann has repeatedly drawn attention (in books such as *Christ and Time* and *The State in the New Testament*) to a neglected area of New Testament studies by pointing out that superhuman forces are mentioned in almost every place where Christ's complete lordship is being discussed. The spirit world is a major factor in the teaching of the whole New Testament. (See Chapter 19 – ed.)

Heinrich Schlier in his book *Principalities and Powers* instances the enormous number of names which the New Testament writers employ to describe this conglomeration of evil forces: they include principalities, power, dominions (*kuriotétes*) thrones, names, princes (*archontes*) lords, gods, angels, spirits, unclean spirits, wicked spirits, elemental spirits (*stoicheia*). This is in addition to the many synonyms for Satan (the devil, the serpent, the lion, the strong one, the wicked one, the accuser, the tempter, the adversary, the enemy, the liar, the murderer, the god of this age, the prince of this world, the prince of the power of the air, Beelzebub and Beliar).

This astonishing collection of names indicates a number of things. First, concern with these spiritual forces was a very important matter to the New Testament writers, and continued to be in the subapostolic age.

Second, despite the variety in nomenclature, the overall picture is the same throughout the Bible, a variety of evil forces under a unified head. It would be foolish and misleading to try to separate the principalities and powers of the Pauline letters from the demons of the Gospels.

Third, the very number and variety of the names for these things shows us that the New Testament writers, unlike their Jewish and pagan predecessors, had no interest in building up demonologies; they enumerated at random, only in order to show that these enemy forces were one and all disarmed by Jesus Christ.

Fourth, the prevalence of this belief in the demonic throughout the ancient world is significant. In Schlier's words, 'In some way revelation absorbed these phenomena from the tradition of universal human experience' (*op. cit.* p. 13). Nowhere does Jesus have to explain himself when exorcising, either on Jewish or Gentile soil. The same applies to the apostles. And the same is true in the subapostolic age. Justin is typical. He castigates those who 'yielding to unreasoning passion and the instigation of demons' persecute the Christians. He is at pains to point out that what the heathen call gods are demonic spirits, and shows how when Socrates tried to make this plain 'the demons themselves, by means of men who rejoiced in wickedness, procured his death as an atheist and a profane person on the charge that he was introducing 'new divinities'; which is just what they do in our case' (*1 Apol.* 5, cf. 14:1, 44:12, *Dial.* 18:3).

Their source and habitation

These principalities and powers are regularly portrayed as the subordinates of the quintessential spirit of evil, Satan himself. In Matthew 25:41 Jesus speaks of 'the devil and all his angels,' clearly indicating demonic powers. In Revelation 16:13, 14 it is plain that demons and unclean spirits are identical: they are lieutenants of Satan. The Beelzebub controversy puts the matter beyond doubt (Matt. 12:22–29). The Pharisees charged Jesus with casting out demons through Beelzebub, the prince of demons, and Jesus rebutted their charge. But both parties were agreed on the nature of these unclean spirits: they derive from the Unholy Spirit himself.

These mighty forces are not merely powerful; they are power. That is, their name and definition: 'dominion,' 'power,' 'might,' and 'authority.' They are said to inhabit 'the air' or 'the heavenly places' (Eph. 2:2, 6:12). How much we should read into these rather vague cosmological statements it is hard to know. But Paul certainly does not simply mean by 'the heavenlies' the home of God, but the surroundings of the material world. They interpenetrate the climate of a country, the *Tendenz* of its politics and the *nuances* of its culture.

Their nature

In recent years a substantial debate has arisen about the nature of these principalities and powers. There has been a tendency to demythologise the concept, and regard them not as fallen spiritual beings but rather as the structures of earthly existence – the state, class struggle, propaganda, international corporations and the like, when they become either tyrannical or objects of man's total allegiance. This has the double attraction of divesting ourselves of belief in so unfashionable a concept as a hierarchy of angels, good and evil, stretching between man and God; it also enables us to find a good deal more in the New Testament about our very modern preoccupation with social structures. Often this debate has been conducted more on the basis of presupposition than of exegesis.

The truth of the matter is that words like principalities, powers and thrones are used both of human rulers and of the spiritual forces which lie behind them. This is readily demonstrable. Lk. 12:11 clearly refers to men when it says, 'When they bring you before the synagogues and the rulers and authorities.' Acts 4:26 equally obviously indicates men, 'The kings of the earth set themselves in array and the rulers were gathered together, against the Lord and against his Anointed.' On the other hand, it is perfectly manifest that the powers and thrones and authorities in Col. 1:16, 2:15, Rom. 8:38, Eph. 6:12 are superhuman powers. There are some passages which could be taken either way, notably 1 Cor. 2:8, Titus 3:1, Romans 13:1. Probably the ambiguity is deliberate.

It is important, then, to realise the flexibility of such terms as principalities, and powers in the usage of the New Testament. They do, on occasion, refer to human authorities. They do, for the main part, refer to superhuman agencies in the spiritual world. And even here there is ambiguity. The most probable interpretation of these powers in Ephesians 1:21f, 3:10 is that they refer to angelic spirits in the court of heaven. The certain interpretation of these powers in Ephesians 2:1f, 6:12f is that they are demonic spirits under Satan's control. And yet the same words are used! It is perhaps an implicit reminder that all power is ultimately God's, and that the fallen spirits were angels before they fell, which is, of course, the consistent teaching of the Bible.

Their influence

The New Testament attributes a widespread influence to these principalities and powers.

1) We see it in the realm of illness. The woman with 'a spirit of infirmity eighteen years who was bowed together and could

not look up' was described by Jesus as 'this daughter of Abraham whom Satan has bound' (Lk. 13:16). The dumb man of Matthew 9:32 was suffering from a demon, and when Jesus had cast it out he was free to speak. In Lk. 9:42 epilepsy is attributed to demonic interference, and in Matthew 12:22 blindness.

2) We see it in some historical situations. 'Behold, the devil will cast some of you into prison' warns the Book of Revelation, and refers to the place 'where Satan's seat is' (Rev. 2:10, 13). Since this was written to Pergamum, the seat of political power in Roman Asia, we are surely right in seeing that Satan had a particular grip of that historical situation. It was the place where 'My faithful witness, Antipas' was martyred for his loyalty to Christ in the midst of political pressures to secede. And who can doubt that such massive extirpations of millions of mankind such as our generation has been in many parts of the world is demonic?

3) We see the influence of the principalities and powers in nature. The whole mythological figure of chaos and leviathan in the Old Testament is an expression of the demonic. So apparently is the incident of Jesus' walking on the water and stilling the storm. He says, 'Peace, be still' (literally, 'Be muzzled') as if to a living entity, the spiritual force which was whipping up that storm into a welter of destruction.

4) We see the principalities and powers in even the Jewish law, as G.B. Caird shows in *Principalities and Powers*, chapter two. So much so that the law which was intended by God for the life of the hearers became their death warrant (Rom. 7:10–14). It had ceased to be understood as the expression of God's love and faithfulness to his people and had become their justification for nomism. To this extent the law given by angels had fallen under the hand of the Enemy who encourages self-righteousness and self-seeking.

5) Christians are certainly not exempt from the principalities and powers. Paul speaks of 'false apostles' who have entered into his churches, disguising themselves as apostles of Christ. 'And no wonder, for even Satan disguises himself as an angel of light. So it is not strange if his servants also disguise

184

themselves as servants of righteousness' (2 Cor. 11:13–15). And heresy, which is incipient throughout the New Testament period, is assigned unambiguously to their agency. 'Do not believe every spirit,' urges John in 1 John 4:1. 'The Spirit expressly says that in the last times some will depart from the faith by giving heed to seducing spirits and doctrines of demons' (1 Tim. 4:1). Christian teaching and Christian teachers alike are subject to attack and distortion by the principalities and powers.

6) Behind human sin there is the activity of these evil forces. 'I can't think what made me do it,' we exclaim, surprised at the reservoirs of evil within us. 'It is not I who do it, but sin which dwells in me,' claimed Paul, reflecting on the force beyond himself which held him in captivity even when he wanted to do the right thing. Such is the human tragedy of Romans 7. Give too much emphasis to this force outside of us, and you rob human beings of responsibility, and make them mere pawns in a celestial tug of war between God and the devil. Give too little weight to it, and you fail to explain the persistent and overwhelming wickedness of mankind, individually and collectively.

7) The state is obviously susceptible to the influence of the principalities and powers. How could it be otherwise when the state is in control of all the other power structures under it? We shall be looking at this later on, but the point is obvious enough whether you think of the Mafia or the Central Intelligence Agency; of the multinationals or the corruption of the police; of the fruitless deadlock between management and labour in England or the endless succession of administrations in Italy. Inflation and unemployment, the arms race and the corruption of morals, these are all manifestations in the modern state of the principalities and powers. The state does not want these things, for the most part. It struggles hard to get rid of them. But it fails. It is in the grip of a power beyond its own.

The Defeat of the Principalities and Powers

1 John 3:8 has a very succinct summary of the reason for the coming of Jesus Christ. 'The reason the Son of God appeared

was to destroy the works of the devil.' That takes us to the heart of the matter. It helps to account for the tremendous burst of satanic activity that faces us in the Gospels, and supremely on the cross. During those thirty odd years the key battle of the history of the universe was being conducted, and both sides knew it.

The triumph of Jesus Christ at the very juncture over the powers and principalities of evil is a major theme of the New Testament. He was tested by persecution at his birth and throughout his life. He was tested by false friends, by hostile religious leaders, by Jewish and Gentile civil authorities. He was tested in the healings, the exorcisms, the temptations in the wilderness. The principalities and powers attacked him through opposition from within his own circle. His own family assigned his notoriety to the devil (Mk. 3:20–35) and one of his intimate friends sold him for thirty pieces of silver. No man was ever tested like Jesus Christ. He faced it all, and overcame it all, as no man before or since has done. The secret of his life was his determination to please his heavenly Father at all points (John 8:29). The spirits of disobedience had never before in the history of mankind discovered a person who was both totally obedient and totally fulfilled in that obedience. No wonder they could get no grip on him. No wonder the demons felt threatened at the very presence of Jesus: 'Have you come here to torment us before the time?' (Matt. 8:29). The evil spirits perceived the ultimate judgment, and they realised that in Jesus Christ the end-time had broken in – and that his appearance in the world spelt their doom.

Three aspects of the cross of Christ

But it was at the cross that Jesus Christ won the greatest and most conclusive victory over the powers of evil. He destroyed their sovereignty over man by utterly submitting to it all the way to the scaffold. In submitting he conquered; just as, conversely, in rebelling they had fallen. Unlike Satan, unlike the powers, unlike Adam, Jesus had not considered being equal with God as a thing to be seized.

Back in 1951 Professor James Stewart made a plea in the *Scottish Journal of Theology* for a recovery of the dimension of the cosmic battle in our theology. Nowhere, he maintained, is it more important than in understanding the meaning of the cross of Christ. He showed how each of the three major factors which led Christ to Golgotha is illuminated by giving full weight to the influence of the invisible cosmic powers.

Behind the cross there lay, first and foremost, the design of man. Basic human failings like pride, jealousy, and greed combined with the self-righteousness and traditionalism of Jewish religion, the injustice of Roman politics, and the apathy of the crowd to take Christ to that gibbet. But behind these religious, political and social pressures stood the principalities and powers of evil. Thus organised religion was there at the cross: all the more dangerous because masquerading as true religion. Politics were there at the cross: but behind Herod and Pilate, the earthly rulers (*archontes*) lay the invisible powers (*archontes*) and it was they who crucified the Lord of glory (1 Cor. 2:8).

Second, behind the cross there lay the will of Jesus himself. He chose with his eyes open. He came to give his life a ransom for many. But here again we are driven to look deeper. Why was it necessary? Because of the grip the strong man had upon the house: the stronger than the strong was needed to set the place free. It was only be facing these forces in the place where they exercised their power that he could break that power. The cross was that place of victory over all the forces of the Enemy. By submitting in perfect obedience right up to death, he broke the power of him who held men in thraldom through its dread. In that cross he conquered.

Third, behind the cross there lay the predestination of God. If God ever acted in history he acted then. But look deeper. In that will of God we see not only his reconciliation of sinners but the complete rebuttal of dualism. These principalities and powers which thwart his will are not independent military units opposing his own army. They are rebel forces of his own. In Christ they were created (Col. 1:16) and in Christ they were defeated (Col. 2:15). Phil. 2:10 makes it quite plain that they must own his sway whether they like it or not. His lordship, since the resurrection, has been beyond cavil among beings celestial, terrestrial and subterranean. 'In the end,' writes Stewart, 'the same invisible powers are the tribute which the Son hands over to the Father, that "God may be all in all."' He concludes this short but important article by pointing out that our real battle is not 'with Communism or Caesarism but with the invisible realm where sinister forces stand flaming and fanatic against the rule of Christ. And the only way to meet that demonic mystic passion is with the passion of the Lord.'

There is little doubt that Stewart has stressed a critical aspect in the cross of Christ, one to which Gustav Aulen has drawn attention in his *Christus Victor*. The power of Satan was shattered on that cross, shattered by the invincible power of love. 'Now is the judgment of this world, when the prince of this world will be cast out,' said Jesus as he faced the cross (John 12:30, cf. 16:11, 14:30). And I think Stewart is right in seeing a studied ambivalence in the 'rulers' of 1 Cor. 2:8. It refers both to Herod and Pilate on the one hand and to the invisible powers on the other. They worked hard to get the Lord of glory on the cross. But in so doing they overreached themselves, and lost the battle. Had they known the outcome they would never have conspired to bring Calvary about.

On the cross the principalities and powers incurred the defeat that indicates the outcome of the whole war, but what is their present condition?

The Present Status of the Principalities and Powers

Since Scripture is not very explicit on this matter, it may be safest to proceed by way of some negatives.

It is not the case that their defeat is only provisional until the last day, as if some theoretical transfer of power has taken place which does not affect anybody or anything. In the coming, the cross and the resurrection of Christ even the greatest of the powers, death, has been affected. And to concentrate on that particular power may help us see what Christ's victory has done to the others. Men still die. Of course they do, and to that extent the power of death is still operative. But the New Testament maintains that death is a defeated foe. It has been robbed of its fangs. Sin, its major adjunct, has been forgiven for the believer, and therefore death no longer has the dread of final separation from the God who is light and love. Moreover in the resurrection of Jesus we see foreshadowed the destiny of every believer: we shall be with him, and we shall be like him (1 Cor. 15:20, 1 John 3:2). In these two respects death has been shorn of its terrors, though we still have to go through it. We know that, evil power and enemy though it is, our Lord holds the key to its defeat and ultimate annihilation.

It is not the case that the principalities and powers have lost their grip on the cosmos at large. True, they have received their death blow, but like a thirty-foot conger with its throat cut which continues for hours thrashing about in a fishing boat, the principalities and powers refuse to lie down and die. They are willing to admit defeat only when faced with the name of Jesus Christ. He is the conqueror and they are vulnerable only when approached on the ground of his victory.

Yet it is not the case that the principalities and powers continue just as they were before the cross of Christ. Their defeat is indeed hidden at present, but they are nevertheless passing away, *katargoumenoi*, as Paul puts it in 1 Cor. 2:6. They have no other expectation than final ruin. And this produces an increasing tempo of chaos; could that be why Jesus forecast wars, rumours of wars and men's heart failing them for fear as the end approached? As time runs out, the atmosphere of history is increasingly filled with the fear of time. Man forgets his transience and dreams of eternity, while the devil knows he has lost eternity and rages at the ever shortening span of time open to him. 'Rejoice O Heaven, and you that dwell therein. But woe to you, O earth and sea, for the devil has come down to you in great rage because he knows that his time is short' (Rev. 12:12).

Therefore it is not the case that things will get better and better and a millennium be created by man on earth. Such facile optimism whether based on Communist, evolutionary or humanistic presuppositions is totally at odds not only with the news but with the teaching of the Bible, which indicates that things will get worse and worse, and men's hearts will cry out for fear. The events prophesied by Jesus in Mark 13, the preoccupations with the loss of time, the tensions between men and nations, the willingness to believe propaganda, the very tremors of the world itself are all manifestations of the frenzied kickings of the satanic bull in God's net as the rope gets drawn tighter. Nor is it surprising that the attacks of the Enemy are primarily directed against the church, whether through heresy from within or seduction or persecution from without. For in the church, however heavily veiled, the principalities and powers discern the person of their conqueror, the Lord Christ. The powers of the age to come are already at work in her, frail and fallible though she is. And as such she reminds the principalities and powers of their doom.

For doom is what awaits them. There is no hint in Scripture that all will come right in the end for the principalities and powers of evil, and for their satanic master. All that offends will be wiped out and will not come into the eternal city (Rev. 21:27). It is not the principalities and powers that have been reconciled by the death of Christ. They have been despoiled, and the church has been reconciled. They have been defeated and the church has been brought out of the power of Satan unto God. The focus of Christ's victory is not to be sought in the principalities and powers but in the church, in those who believe. The genial generosity of those who, like Alan Richardson, maintain that the rebellious powers of evil are in the end to be saved has neither logic nor Scripture to commend it.

The rebellious spirits have locked themselves in a hell which is chained both by their own choice on the inside, and by God on the outside. As Milton, with prophetic insight and poetic brilliance shows in *Paradise Lost*, the great debate between Satan's followers is how to find a way out of that situation other than the one way which exists, the way of repentance and restitution, against which they have resolutely set their faces. But there is no other way. Moloch uses the weapon of blind rage: anything is better than the frustration and agony of fallenness. Belial uses the weapon of caution: gradual acclimatisation to alienation is better than a traumatic reliving of the great rebellion. And Mammon seeks a solution by trying to make hell a substitute for heaven. Indeed, one wonders whether he had really seen the difference between the two! The way of rage, of getting used to one's lot, of blind substitution sometimes works on this earth. But in the ultimacy of the Beyond, Milton knows it cannot be so. Hell is their dungeon, not their safe retreat (2:317).

If logic points this way, so too does Scripture. It does not see the conquered as some scholars have seen them: not tamed and domesticated to do the will of Jesus Christ. They have indeed to confess his sway (Phil 2:10). The archetypal sinners of Gen. 6:3 have heard the proclamation of his achievement (1 Pet. 3:18ff). But rebels they remain, like many of mankind whom they control (Rev. 9:20, 21). A great bottomless pit is reserved for the devil and his angels: so is the lake of fire. And at the end the satanic trinity are found in this place of final ruin while the heavenly Trinity rejoice with the Bride, the church, for ever (Rev. 20:2f, 14, and compare 21:1ff). The destiny of the forces of evil is destruction. They are given over to the ruin which they have chosen and which they propagate. The end is inescapable: any other would be unjust. It is the logical and necessary outcome of the victory already gained through the cross and resurrection. That is why Christians can lift up their heads, however black the clouds. Their hope does not rest upon fairy tales and the hope of pie in the sky, but rather on the solid achievements of Bethlehem, Golgotha and the first Easter Day.

The Subjection of the Invisible Powers

by Oscar Cullmann

Long recognized as one of Europe's top ranking New Testament scholars, Oscar Cullmann here argues, with admirable tenacity and attention to details, that supernatural principalities, powers, rulers, thrones, lordships and other angelic powers stand behind human governments. The fact that some of these powers may be demonic and hostile, Cullmann insists, does not lead us to a heretical dualism which would see demonic powers as having an existence independent of God. Rather, all angelic beings have been created by God and ultimately are subject to their Creator, although God has allowed them to exercise certain moral freedom in this age.

*   *   *   *   *

In 1 Cor. 2:8, in the course of his discussion concerning the 'wisdom' destined by God unto our glory, Paul writes that the rulers of this world had not recognized this wisdom. 'For had they recognized it, they would not have crucified the Lord of glory.' By 'the rulers of this age' Paul manifestly means *both* the invisible 'princes of this world,' who are often mentioned as such, and their actual human instruments, Herod and Pilate. We thereby are directed to an eminently important relation, which gives us the key for the deeper understanding of the problem of redemptive history and history. This problem we now take up.

The assertion that God is also the creator of the invisible things – an assertion taken up in to the later Church confessions of faith in the Orient, as, for example, the Niceno-Constantinopolitan one known from the liturgy of the Mass – has its foundation in the New Testament. On the other hand, we have established the fact that Primitive Christianity does not stop with this statement concerning the creation of the *invisibilia*, but proclaims the victory of Christ over these powers, and we have shown that they are particularly mentioned in every place where his complete Lordship is being discussed.

The existence of these powers Paul regards as certain, even if they have no significance as mediators between God and us (1 Cor. 2:8). As far as their character is concerned, he indeed presupposes much as known, since he here is dealing with views current in late Judaism. His readers obviously know better than we do what is meant when he speaks of 'principalities, powers, rulers, thrones, lordships.' Hence we should pay more attention than is usually given to the late Jewish teaching concerning these angelic powers.

It is connected with an arbitrary distinction between central and peripheral statements of the New Testament when, in the commentaries and presentations of New Testament theology, this entire complex of questions is regarded as more or less unimportant, as nothing but a framework 'conditioned by the contemporary situation.' We must repeat here that there is but one objective criterion for determining what is essential, namely, the earliest formulas of faith. We have seen, however, that in these quite brief summaries of the Primitive Christian revelation the invisible powers are almost invariably mentioned. Whatever our personal attitude toward this view may be, we must conclude from this fact that these powers, in the faith of

Primitive Christianity, did not belong merely to the framework 'conditioned by the contemporary situation.' It is these invisible beings who in some way – not, to be sure, as mediators, but rather as executive instruments of the reign of Christ – *stand behind what occurs in the world.*

We must regard the late Jewish teaching concerning the angels, and especially concerning the angels of the peoples, as belonging to the solid content of faith in the New Testament.

It is the merit of Martin Dibelius that in *Die Geisterwelt im Glauben des Paulus*, 1909, he pointed out for the first time the importance of the faith, widespread in Judaism, that there is a particular angel for each people. Günther Dehn, in his essay, 'Engel und Obrigkeit, ein Beitrag zum Verständnis von Röm. 13:1–7' (in the testimonial volume, *Theologische Aufsätze für Karl Barth*, 1936), has taken up this reference and developed it in greater detail.

This abundantly attested late Jewish belief that all peoples are ruled through angels is present particularly in *The Book of Daniel*, in *The Wisdom of Jesus, Son of Sirach*, and in the *Book of Enoch*, and it can be shown to be present also in the *Talmud* and *Midrash*. It explains the fact that in the already mentioned Ps. 110 the subjection of the pagan enemies of Israel which is there promised to the king of Israel can be unhesitatingly referred to the invisible powers. This faith further explains how, in the well-known ancient confessional psalm, Phil. 2:10, the Old Testament saying of Isa. 45:22f., 'To me every knee shall bow,' which originally had in view the Gentiles, could be referred to the 'beings in heaven, on earth, and in the underworld.'

We understand on the basis of this faith how the existing earthly political power belongs in the realm of such angelic powers. They stood behind the State authorities which had brought Christ to the cross. They are the 'rulers of this age,' whom we mentioned at the beginning of this chapter. Moreover, 1 Cor. 6:3 proves that according to the Primitive Christian view these invisible angelic powers stand behind the earthly states. For it is only on this assumption that it has any meaning when Paul justifies his admonition to the Church, to avoid the

State courts in trials among Christians, by reference to the fact that the members of the Church will judge the 'angels' at the end of the days.

Thus the so-called 'Christological grounding of the State' is not at all based, as is usually presupposed by the opponents of this view, merely upon the interpretation given to the 'authorities' of Rom. 13:1. It is based rather upon the very specific late Jewish teaching concerning the angels of the peoples; this teaching is taken up into Primitive Christianity and actually plays there a very important role in connection with the significance that attaches to the *subjection of the angelic powers through Christ*.

Therefore it will not do to transfer this conception of the angels and powers to the periphery of the Pauline theology, as is done by G. Kittel, and by F.J. Leenhardt. On these and other grounds they reject the reference of the 'authorities' of Rom 13:1 to angelic powers.

The famous passage Rom. 13:1ff. contains rather a confirmation of this conception. We shall see that only when this conception is found there does the entire section become really clear; only then does it fall into harmony with the entire outlook of Paul.

For everyone who comes from the other Pauline passages to Rom. 13:1 and considers it without prejudice, uninfluenced by the usage of the word in secular history and by the familiar translation into modern languages, it is by far the most natural thing to give to the plural ἐξουσίαι no other sense than that which it always has for Paul, that is, the meaning of 'angelic powers.'

When G. Kittel argues against this that in some eighty out of ninety instances where the New Testament has the word ἐξουσία, we find only the ordinary meaning of 'any power which someone has,' it must be replied that this usage of the singular is not under discussion here. We here are dealing with the *plural form* ἐξουσίαι or with the pluralistic usage of the singular πᾶσα ἐξουσία ('all authority'), and with reference to it the result of New Testament statistical study is quite clear.

To be sure, it becomes crystal-clear from the context that the passage is speaking of the State. This, however, only proves that the conception that we have found in the other two Pauline passages and that is abundantly attested for late Judaism is also found here, the view, namely, that the actual State authority is thought of as the executive agent of angelic powers. The fact that in ordinary Greek usage the singular and the plural (even when used together with ἀρχαί, 'principalities') designate only the earthly magistracy, may not be cited in proof of the view that also in Rom. 13:1ff. only this meaning can be considered. The ordinary Greek usage is not familiar with the late Jewish and New Testament teaching concerning the angelic powers. Accordingly, and as a matter of course, the corresponding use of the word ἐξουσίαι is also foreign to it. But that Paul, for whom this word elsewhere always designates angelic powers, think of them here too, but specifically as *the invisible angelic powers that stand behind the State government*, is naturally suggested by the very use of the word in secular history, a usage that was indeed known also to him and with which he connected the late Jewish and New Testament usage. Thus as a result the term has for Paul a double meaning, which in the case corresponds exactly to the content, since the State is indeed the executive agent of invisible powers.

The analogy to 1 Cor. 2:8 is complete with respect not only to content but also to language. For here also, where it is quite plain that by ἄρχοντες τοῦ αἰῶνος τούτου are meant both the invisible 'rulers of this age' *and* the visible ones, Pilate and Herod, there stands in characteristic fashion a term that in secular Greek naturally designates only the actual human rulers, while in the New Testament it designates also the invisible ones. In 1 Cor. 2:8 as well as in Rom. 13:1 the expressions are purposely so chosen that they make clear the *combined meaning* that is typical of the conception we have indicated.

This explanation of ἐξουσίαι, which is quite compelling, was represented later in antiquity, outside of the New Testament, by Gnostics in their interpretation of Rom. 13:1; this we learn through Irenaeus (*Against Heresies*, V,24,1). To be sure, we know nothing more definite concerning their interpretation of the entire passage. It is probable that these heretics, in the context of their dualistic outlook, conceived these 'authorities' that stand behind the State simply as evil powers and nothing more; in this case, to be sure, it is not clear how they may have interpreted the demand of Paul for obedience to those powers.

In any case, it is an established fact that Irenaeus himself, the opponent of the Gnostics, only rejected the interpretation of 'authorities' as angelic powers because he took into consideration merely this false dualistic understanding, and on this view to interpret the 'authorities' to mean the invisible powers that stand behind the State would make of this State itself an institution hostile to God. The New Testament conception of 'authorities,' however, is definitely not dualistic in this sense. By their subjection under Christ the invisible powers have rather lost their evil character, and they also now stand under the within the Lordship of Christ, as long as they are subject to him and do not seek to become emancipated from their place in his service. Since Irenaeus probably, like his Gnostic opponents, reckons only with a false dualistic conception of the angelic powers, he must reject as heretical the connection with them of the 'authorities' of Rom. 13:1.

In the Primitive Christian faith in the conquest of the invisible powers through Christ, the significant thing is the very fact that while this faith holds firmly to the existence of powers originally hostile to God, it nevertheless does not concede to this existence any independent significance, and so it avoids all dualism. The strongly Christocentric attitude is in no way endangered by this faith; 'even if there are such beings,' Paul writes in 1 Cor. 8:5f., 'Yet *we* have only *one* God and *one* Lord.' To him, indeed, all these powers are now subjected. They are bound. That which the Apocalypse of John says of the binding of Satan in the end time (Rev. 20:2) holds true somehow for the Pauline conception of the present situation of the angelic powers. In the time between the resurrection and the Parousia of Christ they are, so to speak, bound as to a rope, which can be more or less lengthened, so that those among them who show tendencies to emancipation can have the illusion that they are releasing themselves from their bond with Christ, while in reality, by this striving which here and there appears, they only show more their original demonic character; they cannot, however, actually set themselves free. Their power is only an apparent power. The Church has so much the more the duty to stand against them, in view of the fact that it knows that their power is only apparent and that in reality Christ has already conquered all demons.

A certain freedom, however, is left to the angelic powers within their subject position. This explains how, in the present stage of redemptive history, it still is not possible for the Church to take without qualification or criticism the view that the State is divine, even though, on the other hand, the State too belongs within the Lordship of Christ. The situation is thus in this respect quite complex, and every simplifying presentation of it fails even in this point to do justice to the Primitive Christian conception. The complexity is connected with that of the entire intermediate situation of the present time. On the one side, the angelic powers are already subjected, and in this respect are placed in the service of Christ, so that of them it can be said in the most positive manner that although they had formerly been enemies they have now become 'ministering spirits sent forth for ministry' (Heb. 1:14); hence obedience toward them is demanded from the Christians in Rom. 13:1ff., where their agents are designated by precisely the same expressions as 'God's minister' (Rom. 13:4) and as 'servants of God' (Rom. 13:6). On the other side, however, the apostle Paul still remains critical toward this State; the Christians should keep away from the state courts and settle their cases among themselves (1 Cor. 6:1ff). Not so very much later the same Roman state of which Paul speaks so positively in Rom., ch. 13, can be designated the 'beast' by another New Testament writer (Rev. 13:1ff).

This apparently contradictory attitude extends through the entire New Testament. But of this contradiction also it holds good that it appears as such only for him who has not recognized the complexity of the situation in the redemptive history. We have seen that this complexity has its roots in a temporal but not in a metaphysical dualism. We know the ground of this temporal dualism. That tension between present and future, between 'already fulfilled' and 'not yet completed,' which contains the key to the understanding of the entire New Testament, shows itself when applied to our problem in the fact that the angelic powers are already made the 'footstool' of the feet of Christ, and yet must once more be overcome at the end. The Kingdom of Christ is indeed already present; in it both areas, the Church and the world, are placed under Christ; nevertheless they are distinguished, since they will merge into one only in the Kingdom of God, when at the end Christ's mediatorial role has been fulfilled (1 Cor. 15:28).

If in the 'authorities' of Rom. 13:1 as well as in the 'rulers of this age' of 1 Cor. 2:8 we see both the invisible powers and their executive agents on earth, there results a completely unified view of the State in the New Testament, and the apparent contradiction within Paulinism between 1 Cor. 6:1ff. and Rom. 13:1ff, or the still greater one within the New Testament between Rev., ch. 13, and Rom., ch. 13, vanishes. For it becomes discernible that, in spite of all the positive statements of Rom. 13:1ff., the State here, as in the entire Primitive Christian conception, is not an ultimate but only a penultimate institution, which will vanish when this age does; the Christian believer will always place over against the State a final question mark and will remain watchful and critical, because he knows that behind it stand powers which do indeed have their place in the divine order determined by the victory of Christ, but which nevertheless for the time being still have a certain possibility of permitting their demonic strivings for independence to flare up into apparent power.

This commissioning of the State has as result that the State agrees with the Christian Church in its judgment concerning good and evil (v. 3f.). Indeed, recompense, punishment, and reward presuppose the capacity for this judgment. This agreement Paul simply confirms; the State rewards the good and punishes the evil. This accord with the Church in spite of the completely opposed fundamental position – here recompense, there love – comes from the fact that the State stands in a divine order in which it becomes the agent of the divine recompense. How important this concept of the divine 'order' (τάξεις) is to the apostle appears at the beginning of the chapter in the heaping up of the words that contain this root: ὑποτάσσεσθαι ('be subject'), τεταγμένος ('ordained'), anti-tássomai ('resist'), διαταγή ('ordinance'). We thus confirm the fact that even apart from the significance of the word 'authorities' in Rom., ch. 13, a view is here presupposed according to which the State, not by nature, but only by its being placed in a definite order, is God's servant and fulfills his will.

In this case, however, the context yields a complete confirmation of the interpretation, much disputed in recent years, that the 'authorities' are the subjected angelic powers. On the other hand, this interpretation gives to the entire section a particular emphasis; it does so by giving the section a place in the article of faith, so very important for the Primitive Church, concerning the subjection of all invisible angelic powers; it thus builds the State into the structure of that order which Primitive Christianity regards as *present sovereign reign of Christ*. The so-called 'Christological foundation' of the State is thereby proved to be correct. It is in the position to explain satisfactorily the parrallelism of 1 Cor. 6:1ff. and Rom. 13:1ff, and on the other hand of Rom. 13:1ff. and Rev., ch. 13, which all refer to the same Roman State. The angelic powers are placed in the service of the Kingdom of Christ, not by their original nature, but only by being bound; they are, however, elevated to the highest dignity by the function that is here assigned to them. Nevertheless, they can for a time free themselves from their bound condition and then show their demonic character. But the final Christian criticism of the State can never be omitted, not even where a State remains in its completely bound situation; because in its original nature it is not divine, it can never be regarded as an ultimate fact. Hence the negative attitude in 1 Cor. 6:1ff. toward so completely legitimate an institution as the State courts of justice. In view of this passage, which is also Pauline, Rom. 13:1ff. cannot and must not be understood in so uncritical and unthinking a way as is often the case. Neither of the two passages may be explained without reference to the other.

The 'Christological foundation' of the State which is here championed has been accused of making the subjection of the powers simply identical with a 'commissioning.' Yet, it is objected, the new Testament speaks only of a subjection. This, however, is not quite correct. As we have seen, the Epistle to the Hebrews in particular speaks, in a way similar to late Jewish teaching concerning angels, of the 'ministering spirts sent forth to minister' ($\lambda\epsilon\iota\tau\text{ov}\varrho\gamma\iota\varkappa\grave{\alpha}$ $\pi\nu\epsilon\acute{v}\mu\alpha\tau\alpha$ $\epsilon\grave{\iota}\varsigma$ $\delta\iota\alpha\varkappa\text{ov}\acute{\iota}\alpha\nu$ $\mathring{\alpha}\pi\text{o}\sigma$-$\tau\epsilon\lambda\lambda\acute{o}\mu\epsilon\nu\alpha$; Heb. 1:14). In this connection it seems to me particularly noteworthy that in this passage these 'ministering spirits' are expressly whom the Christ who sits at the right hand of God 'makes the footstool of his feet.' And it is furthermore of the greatest significance that precisely in our section of the thirteenth chapter of Romans, introduced with the mention of the 'authorities,' we find applied to these 'authorities' who stand behind the actual State the same expressions 'minister' ($\delta\iota\acute{\alpha}\varkappa\text{ov}\text{o}\varsigma$; v. 4) and 'ministers' ($\lambda\epsilon\iota\tau\text{ov}\varrho\gamma\text{o}\acute{\iota}$; v. 6), that are contained in the designation of the subjected powers in The Epistle to the Hebrews.

We thus come to the conclusion that the relation that we have indicated between the State and angelic powers agrees in every respect with the little that we hear concerning the State in the New Testament.

Index